INSIGHT POCKET GUIDE

Cancún
The Yucatán

Discovery CHANNEL

APA PUBLICATIONS
Part of the Langenscheidt Publishing Group

Mexico
320 kilometers / 200 miles
UNITED STATES
Gulf of Mexico
Pacific Ocean
Golfo de California
Bahía de Campeche
Golfo de Tehuantepec
Golfo de Honduras
Mississippi Delta
Tijuana
Mexicali
Tecate
Ensenada
Casa Grande
Gila
Tucson
Roswell
Lubbock
Red
Texarkana
Mississippi
Birmingham
Las Cruces
Carlsbad
Abilene
Brazos
Fort Worth
Dallas
Jackson
Mobile
Baton Rouge
New Orleans
San Quintín
Caborca
Nogales
Ciudad Juárez
Magdalena
Colorado
Austin
Houston
Punta Prieta
Nuevo Casas Grandes
Rio Grande
Rio Bravo del Norte
San Antonio
Rosarito
Hermosillo
Yaqui
Chihuahua
Delicias
Salado
San Ignacio
Santa Rosalia
Ciudad Obregón
Nueva Rosita
Corpus Christi
Jiménez
Sierra Madre Oriental
Sierra Madre Occidental
Fuerte
Nuevo Laredo
Loreto
Hidalgo del Parral
Monclova
Reynosa
Matamoros
Ciudad Constitución
Los Mochis
Torreón
Monterrey
Saltillo
Isla Santa Margarita
La Paz
Culiacán
Todos Santos
Durango
Mazatlán
Matehuala
Ciudad Victoria
Cabo San Lucas
San José del Cabo
Zacatecas
Tecuala
Tampico
Islas Marias
San Luis Potosí
Tepic
Santiago
León
Guanajuato
Poza Rica
Cabo Corrientes
Puerto Vallarta
Guadalajara
Ciudad de Mexico
Jalapa
Islas Revillagigedo
Colima
Iztaccíhuatl 5286
Toluca
Puebla
Veracruz
Cuernavaca
Izúcar de Matamoros
Balsas
Coatzacoalcos
Lázaro Cárdenas
Chilpancingo
Sierra Madre del Sur
Oaxaca
Villahermosa
Acapulco
Pinotepa Nacional
Juchitán
Tuxtla Gutiérrez
Grijalva
Comitán
Usumacinta
Cabo Catoche
Mérida
Cancún
Valladolid
Yucatán
Campeche
Felipe Carrillo Puerto
Escárcega
Chetumal
BELIZE
Belmopan
GUATEMALA
HONDURAS

Welcome!

The name Yucatán has its beginnings in a misunderstanding. When the Spanish conquistadors landed on this tropical peninsula in 1530 they asked the Mayan inhabitants its name. They were told 'Yucatán' and the name stuck. What they didn't know was that Yucatán was actually 'We don't understand you,' in the local Mayan dialect.

In these pages Insight Guides' correspondent in Yucatán ensures that there are no misunderstandings in the minds of modern-day travelers. In 11 carefully crafted itineraries centered around four key bases that encapsulate the best of the Mexican states comprising the peninsula (Quintana Roo, Campeche and Yucatán itself), she roams from the showcase resort of Cancún to the colonial city of Mérida, out-of-the-way Campeche, the pyramids of Chichén-Itzá and Uxmal, and takes a boat to the Isla Mujeres and the divers' Mecca of Cozumel. The tours are carefully paced and include stops for invigorating Cuban-style coffee and tasty Mexican cuisine. Where appropriate, tips are given on where to lodge for the night.

Margaret King has spent over 25 years living and working in Mexico. She frequently travels to the Yucatán Peninsula from her base in Mexico City, lured by her fascination for Mayan civilization as well as the promise of *palapa*-roofed bungalows and tropical seas. One of the things she loves most about the region is its enduring links with the past. The Mayan Indians haven't disappeared, she says. 'People with faces that seem to have come to life from a stone relief or codex book will be your sales clerks, hoteliers, and guides.'

Pages 2/3: Nunnery Quadrangle, Uxmal

C O N T E N T S

History & Culture

Yucatán's Highlights

These 11 itineraries concentrate on the best of the Yucatán Peninsula. They focus on four key bases: Cancún, Chichén-Itzá, Mérida and Campeche, and suggest interesting excursions that can be taken from each.

Pages 8/9: Playa del Carmen

History & Culture

The Yucatán Peninsula, jutting out into the Gulf of Mexico and the Caribbean Sea and reaching to within 320km (200 miles) of the island of Cuba, thrust itself up from the seabed many millions of years ago, rising above the waters like a long-submerged raft. Perhaps a turtle would be a better image, as the Mayas saw the earth as a turtle shell.

Uncounted generations of mollusks, whose crushed and powdered shells layered the ocean floor, became the porous limestone of the peninsula, through which rain quickly filters down to underground rivers and caves. Over time, the roofs of some caverns collapsed, dotting the landscape with water-filled sinkholes. Unlike the soaring tree canopies found to the south, a dense scrub vegetation is all the thin topsoil can support.

Not a particularly promising landscape for human populations, it might seem, but such was not the case. According to recent calculations, people began crossing the Bering Straits some 50,000 years ago, slowly progressing further south over the millennia to Yucatán and beyond. Agriculture began to supplement the food obtained from hunting and gathering in settlements as early as 13,000BC, and the thatch-roofed Mayan dwelling, the *na*, still so typical today, was already in use at least 3,000 years ago.

The Fascinating Maya

By 800–300BC there was extensive trade between coastal peoples and highland groups, exchanging salt from the sea for hard obsidian stone tools produced by highland groups. The Olmec culture to the southwest in what is present-day Tabasco was then at its peak, creating giant stone heads – some 3m (10ft) tall – as well as delicately carved small jade pieces. The Olmecs, regarded by some scholars as the 'mother culture' of subsequent Mesoamerican tribes, left few clues to their civilization beyond this evidence of their sculptural mastery.

By 300BC the Maya, one of the most intriguing, complex and refined of the world's ancient peoples, had emerged: a class of nobility and scribes ruling political and intellectual life, building immense temples and creating elaborately painted ceramics.

Olmec sculpture

Mayan fresco

Not using the wheel for transportation and lacking metal tools, the Maya nevertheless developed a high degree of astronomical knowledge. Making accurate planetary observations through the carefully aligned doors and windows of their temples, they pinpointed the path of the planet Venus to within 20 seconds per year. Time was one of the ruling forces of their entire civilization, since history was considered to repeat itself when celestial circumstances were duplicated. They developed a calendar more accurate than the one we use today and counted time backwards to millions of years, with a seeming grasp of infinity. Their mathematicians developed the concept of zero, a major achievement, which not even the great Pythagoras had been able to comprehend. And although almost no literature has come down – only four codices survived – we can study the Maya through their enormously complicated system of hieroglyphics, which makes extensive use of human faces accompanied by myriad interlocking symbols. Much of it remains undeciphered.

Then there is the architecture – magnificent stone temple and palace complexes, the centerpieces of thriving cities, some reaching populations exceeding 100,000. At the apogee of Mayan civilization, independent city states liberally populated the Yucatán Peninsula, never transforming themselves into the type of empire later developed by the Aztecs of the central plateau. High cultural levels were first achieved in the area of present-day Guatemala at such sites as the glorious Tikal, whose skyscraper pyramids soar above the trees. By the late Classic era, 600–900AD, the centers of culture had shifted to the lowlands of Yucatán, where over the centuries several architectural styles developed, including Puuc (whose proportions were inspired by the Mayan dwelling), Chenes (characterized by huge masks) and Río Bec (a florid development with pyramids and steps so steep they could no longer be ascended). Painting as exemplified by the murals in Bonampak, realistically depicting a post-battle scene, achieved dizzying levels of virtuosity.

Mayan head with sloping forehead

In sculpture, reliefs of human figures were weighed down by symbols, and the people themselves, at least the nobility, transformed their own bodies into works of art. In order to achieve the sharply sloped forehead, wooden plaques were strapped to new-born babies' heads. Teeth were inlaid with valuable stones or filed to points. Judging from the figures shown in paintings and reliefs of kings, Mayan leaders wore complicated headdresses and costumes that made them appear twice their natural size.

But Mayan life was not merely a peaceful synthesis of astronomy, art, and religion. City state warred with city state and outsiders from the highlands invaded the lowland cultures. Around 900AD, the Maya mysteriously abandoned most of their magnificent ceremonial centers and sites and these became so overgrown by the jungle that even their names were forgotten. They remained undisturbed for nearly a thousand years, until their rediscovery by intrepid adventurers in the 19th century. These mostly foreign explorers, perhaps inspired by the unearthing of Pompeii and Napoleon's Egyptian adventures (along with Champollion's subsequent deciphering of the Rosetta stone), endured incredible hardships to reach the lost cities, hacking away the enveloping jungle. A whole lore has grown up around such pioneers as Bostonian John Stephens, whose writings set the standard as the forerunner of serious Maya studies; Britain's Frederick Catherwood, whose intricately detailed drawings are used by today's archeologists; and the French photographer Desiré Charnay, who struggled through the jungles with early camera equipment.

Mayan ruins depicted by Frederick Catherwood

The Spanish Conquest

When the Spanish, establishing a base in Campeche, began their attempt to conquer the Yucatán in 1530, the Maya had been fighting among themselves for hundreds of years. Although never forming an alliance, they nevertheless resisted their invaders so successfully that Francisco de Montejo and his son retreated to Mexico City after four fruitless years. In 1540, the younger Montejo returned and, using the divide-and-conquer strategy employed by Cortés in the highlands nearly 20 years earlier, defeated the Cocom Maya with the enthusiastic cooperation of another Mayan tribe, the Xiu. He founded Mérida in 1542 on the site of the Maya city T'ho and within four years the entire peninsula was at least nominally subject to Spanish rule.

Water-carrier of the colonial era

As elsewhere in lands colonized by Spain, the Catholic Church followed in the footsteps of the soldiers, sending priests to convert the natural inhabitants of the conquered lands. Considering the Mayan writings and religion to be works of Satan, iconoclast Friar Diego de Landa, in the town of Maní in 1562, ordered the burning of 27 hieroglyphic books and 5,000 idols. The Indians who witnessed the act are said to have wailed in anguish as they watched this annihilation of a vital and irreplaceable part of their cultural heritage.

Landa has earned the everlasting reprobation of subsequent generations of scholars who would have found these manuscripts invaluable in piecing together Mayan culture. The friar later wrote the definitive treatise on Mayan customs, and the brief formula for deciphering hieroglyphs that he mentioned almost casually has been a key in the slow work of interpreting the hieroglyphs fortunately left in stone reliefs on hundreds of stelai.

Under Spanish rule, the hapless Indians, reduced to little more than unwilling slaves and lacking resistance to new diseases such as smallpox that the Europeans unwittingly brought with them, died by the tens of thousands. They did, however, receive a measure of protection from the friars sent to convert them, as well as from Spanish law.

Over the three centuries of the colonial period the Yucatán, governed directly from Spain rather than through the viceroys in distant Mexico City, developed a distinct identity of its own, a particular syncretism of the Mayan and Spanish cultures. Isolated from the center of Mexican power and barely participating in the movement to break away from Spanish rule, it did not definitively become part of the young republic until 1848, almost three decades after independence had been won.

A 'nouveau riche' class built grand mansions

New Crops and Nouveaux Riches

With the coming of independence, Yucatán lost its traditional trade markets – Spain, Cuba and Mexico City – so new sources of income had to be found. (The peninsula now comprised the states of Yucatán, Campeche and the territory of Quintana Roo.) Henequen, the agave plant that produces the fiber used in rope, became one solution, although because the plant requires eight years to reach maturity investors were initially scarce. Experimental cultivation began, however, and was eventually to create a class of millionaires whose fortunes were based on what came to be called *el oro verde* (green gold). Production of the fiber increased tenfold between 1879 and 1916, by which time it was known as sisal, named for the only port in northwest Yucatán. Sisal became a thriving industry mainly because the Indians did the work. It was in reality slave labor and that was one of the better-kept secrets of Porfirio Díaz's regime.

Another crop that could now be exploited after the elimination of the Spanish embargo was sugar cane, a more immediately lucrative investment with annual returns of 700 percent after the second year. Land became the key to wealth and so-called empty lots were confiscated, although they had been common lands of the Maya, who like the Indians in the US considered land to be unsellable. Resentment ran high and together with other factors led to the War of the Castes, which broke out in the city of Valladolid in 1847, with Indians killing, raping or enslaving every white person they could find.

By the following year, the only parts of Yucatán not under Maya power were the walled cities of Mérida and Campeche. When, however, victory was imminent for the insurgents, they suddenly abandoned their siege because the appearance of winged ants was interpreted as signalling their annual obligation to sow the lands and propitiate the rain god Chaac, who kept droughts at bay. This task they perceived as their higher obligation, above fighting the Spanish.

Meanwhile the federal government in Mexico City, which had been engaged in battling invading US troops, now turned its attention to Yucatán, sending troops who ended the revolt with such savagery that the Indian population was halved in just seven years (1848–55). Innocents were massacred simply for being Indian and the Maya were sold as slaves to Cuba – at a price of $45 a head for men and $25 for women.

Henequen: 'green gold'

Some rebels took refuge in the inaccessible jungles of neighboring Quintana Roo and a cult grew up, the Chan Santa Cruz group, based on the 'Talking Cross', a melange of the ancient Mayan belief in the cross as symbol of the sacred tree and Christian teachings. The holy voice was actually a ventriloquist who inspired the Indians to continue their fight and issued strategic orders. In 1857 the Talking Cross 'ordered' the Maya – who were equipped with arms and ammunition bought from British traders across the border in Belize – to attack. The time was ripe, for there was rivalry between Mérida and Campeche and squabbling among the whites. The followers of the Talking Cross went on the march against town after town. In three years they had captured 4,000 whites.

It was not until 1934 that the last rebels signed a peace treaty – shortly before Quintana Roo became a territory – and it was another 40 years before it became a state of the Mexican republic. This was in 1974 when Cancún's potential as a tourist destination was realized and the first hotels were opened.

In the 1920s the state's first socialist governor, Felipe Carrillo Puerto, started to take measures to improve the lot of the Maya. He instituted a labor union and, reversing the usual custom of seizing land from the Indians, decreed that abandoned *haciendas* were subject to expropriation.

This, together with his scandalous desertion of his wife in order to live openly with US journalist Alma Reed, earned him the hatred of the conservative moneyed class. When Alma Reed returned to San Francisco for a visit in 1923, Carrillo was assassinated by his enemies. This romantic chapter in history has been immortalized in the song *La Peregrina* (The Wanderer), written at Carrillo's request by the Yucatán composer Ricardo Palmerín. The town where the Talking Cross was located has been renamed Felipe Carrillo Puerto in his honor.

Liquid refreshment: tequila

Tourism: a Boon and a Bane

Today, the Yucatán Peninsula thrives on light industry and tourism. Cancún was developed after a computer study determined that it was the most promising spot on the Caribbean at which to establish a new world-class resort for international tourism, complete with infrastructure for all the townspeople providing services there. The first hotels opened in 1972 and the building has gone on ever since.

Oil is another growth industry. As in southern Veracruz and Tabasco, Campeche is filled with men drilling for oil, which has, inevitably, changed the way of life. There's money floating around and the standard of living for Yucatán's 2 million people is slowly improving. Many pure Maya now have land on which to grow corn and beans and raise cattle. But, on the down side, inflation rides high, and there is a serious pollution problem.

Alarmed, until recently, by rapid encroachment on lands that had been virtually virgin and by the rate at which forests were being destroyed, groups sharing in the Maya heritage are now cooperating in creating biosphere reserves. The aim is to offer economic alternatives to the inhabitants while exploring new approaches to tourism that are both friendly to a rich but fragile environment and bring in much needed income.

Maya scholarship continues with, for example, the discovery of several lost cities in the Calakmul Biosphere Reserve, overlapping Guatemalan territory, and including what may be the tallest Maya pyramid ever built. In the early years of the 21st century, Yucatán faces great challenges, but the will to meet them is strong.

Fishing still thrives

Historical Highlights

3,000BC Former hunters and gatherers become farmers with the Mexican 'trinity' of staples – corn, beans and chillies – already among their main crops.

1,500–200BC Olmec culture develops, blossoms and declines. Considered to have had great influence on later Mayan peoples, the Olmecs are noted for their colossal stone head sculptures.

200–900AD Classical period when many Mesoamerican cultures reach their high point, with the building of large cities and complex ceremonial centers. Chichén-Itzá and Uxmal are among Mayan sites in the Yucatán.

900AD Beginning of post-Classical period when most cities are mysteriously abandoned. Major cultural changes take place.

1325 Founding of Aztec city Tenochtitlán, site of present-day Mexico City.

1511 Shipwrecked Spanish sailors land in Yucatán.

1519–21 Beginning of Hernando Cortés's conquest of Mexico, fall of Tenochtitlán.

1542 The Spanish found the cities of Campeche and Mérida after 20 years of Maya resistance.

1547 First Franciscan monasteries built in Yucatán.

1562 Burning of Maya manuscripts in town of Maní, by order of Friar Diego de Landa, who deemed them works of Satan.

1663 A pirate attack on city of Campeche leads to the building of enclosing walls, making it one of the most heavily fortified settlements in the Americas.

1683 A gang of 2,000 pirates loot Veracruz.

1810–21 Mexican War of Independence from Spain.

1823 Yucatán becomes part of new nation of Mexico, with status of statehood.

1839 and **1842** American John Stephens and British artist Frederick Catherwood make their famous trips to Mexico, Central America and the Yucatán.

1847–51 War of the Castes, a bloody Mayan uprising against the white population, with equally brutal reprisals. Close to a third of the population is wiped out.

1857 The 'Talking Cross' deems time is ripe for new Mayan offensive against whites.

1860 An uneasy truce, lasting 40 years, begins between the Maya and the whites.

1863 Campeche becomes a state.

1915 The Mexican government extracts millions of pesos from Yucatán landowners against Pancho Villa and Emiliano Zapata.

1920 End of 30-year dictatorship of Porfirio Díaz. Mexican revolution, the world's first in the 20th century.

1923 Assassination of Yucatán governor, Felipe Carrillo Puerto. First reconstruction work undertaken in Chichén-Itzá.

1974 Quintana Roo made a Mexican state. First hotels opened in the resort of Cancún, Quintana Roo.

1994, January Indigenous uprising in state of Chiapas under the leadership of the Zapatista Army of National Liberation brings national and world attention to the continuing plight of native peoples.

1994, March Assassination of Luis Donaldo Colosio, presidential candidate of the PRI (Institutional Revolutionary Party).

2000 July elections bring in the PAN (National Action Party), ending 80 years of PRI (Institutional Revolutionary Party) rule.

Yucatán
80 kilometers / 50 miles
Tour 2
Tour 3
Tour 11
Gulf of Mexico
Progreso
Chuburna
Punta Baz
Sisal
PARQUE NATURAL DEL FLAMENCO DE CELESTÚN
Dzibilchaltún
Baca
Punta Boxcohuo
Hunucmá
Mérida
Kinchil
Aké
Celestún
Umán
Hóctun
Bella Flor
Seyé
Chochola
Tekoh
Maxcanu
Mayapán
Oxkintoc
Muna
Tekit
Halacho
Lázaro Cárdenas
Ticul
Calkini
Uxmal
Teabo
Oxkutzcab
Jaina (Zac-Pol)
Punta Nitún
Pochoc
Kabáh
Hecelchacán
Labná
Xcalumkin
Sayil
Pomuch
Ticum
Kihuic
Tenabo
Campeche
Lerma
Start
Boxol
Xkichmook
Chencoyi
Nocuchich
Cayal
Hopelchen
Seyba Playa
Tixmucuy
Balneario Acapulco
Edzná
Nohyaxché
Dzibilnocac
Haltunchén
Pich
Ruíz Cortínes
Dzibalchen
Champotón
Moquel
Hochob
San Enrique
MÉXI
Chencán
Pustunich
Bahía de Campeche
Huayahaca
CAMPECHE
RESERVA DE LA BIÓSFERA DE CALAKMUL
Aquiles Serdan
Puerto Real
Ciudad del Carmen
Ponte Diáz Ordaz
Francisco Escárcega
Zacafal
Laguna de Términos
Mamantal
Lechugal
Lago Sivituc
Dzinapara
Conhuas
Becán
Xpuhil
Chicaná
Fuco Villa
Río Bec
Coyoc
Candelaria
El Ramonal
Palizada
Este
Buenavista
Caribe
Escondido
Tortuga
Chumpan
Maruchín
Candelaria
El Tigre
Calakmul
Cuauhtémoc
Villa El Triunfo
Chable
Playas de Catazajá
Balakbal
GUATEMALA
172
4
281
261
180
18
24
188
186

Río Lagartos
Punta de Bachul
San Felipe
RIO LAGARTOS PARQUE NACIONAL
SAN FELIPE PARQUE NACIONAL
Isla Holbox
Cabo Catoche
Laguna de Yalahán
Isla Contoy
ISLA CONTOY BIRD SANCTUARY
Chiquila
Dzilam de Bravo
Solferino
San Angel
Isla Mujeres
Puerto Juárez
Cancún
Start
Sucila
Kikil
Tizimín
Temax
Xlacah
Culuba
Kantunilkin
Tepakán
Leona Vicario
PUNTA NIZUC MARINE PARK
Izamal
Espita
Ekbalám
Dzitas
Xcan
El Tintal
Puerto Morelos
Kantunil
YUCATÁN
Temozón
Candelaria
Libre Unión
Pisté
Gruta de Balancanché
Valladolid
Playa del Carmen
Punta Bete
Chichén-Itzá
Chemax
Ikil
Xcalacoop
Chichimila
Lago Punta Laguna
Pamul
Punta Molas
Sotuta
Tixcacalcupul
San Miguel de Cozumel
San Gervasio
Yaxuná
Cobá
Akumal
Ixhill
Xcacel
Isla de Cozumel
Xel-Há
El Cedral
Xtobil
Tancah
Finish
Tulúm
Peto
San José
Chunyazche
Tzucacab
Melchor Ocampo
Muyil
La Aguada
Chamax
Dzuiché
Señor
Punta Conoco
Vigía Chico
Punta Allen
José Maria Morelos
Bahia de la Ascensión
Tixmul
Caribbean Sea
QUINTANA ROO
Polyuc
Felipe Carrillo Puerto
Tampak
RESERVA DE LA BIÓSFERA SIAN KA'AN
Punta Santa Rosa
Chan Santa Cruz Poniente
Uhmay
Punta Herrero
Mosquitero
Los Limones
Placer
Tigrito
Pedro Antonio de los Santos
Punta Changuay
Judas Tadeo
Cayo Norte
Laguna Bacalar
Bacalar
Bahia Chetumal
Majahual
Cayo Centro
Banco Chinchorro
Calderitas
Fuco Villa
Chetumal
Kohunlich
Santa Elena
Cayo de Blackford
Cayo Lobos
Buena Vista
BELIZE
Xcalak
Tomás Garrido
San Estevan
Orange Walk
Reef Point
Carmelita
El Posito
Rancho
Azúl
San Pedro
Santana
295
176
180
307
184
186

Cancún

1. Cancún's town and beaches

A leisurely introduction to Cancún, Mexico's prime Caribbean tourist destination, beginning with a tour of the downtown area followed by a drive through the elegant hotel zone. Lunch, then an afternoon on the beach or a trip in a glass-bottomed boat.

Cancún's David Hockney-turquoise sea and powdery white beaches are legendary. Protected by a coral-reef barrier, the waters seem like a giant pool; the mood is gentle, tropical. When the 19th-century American explorer John Stephens sailed past in the early 1840s he noted that: 'In the afternoon we steered for the mainland, passing the island of Kancune, a barren strip of land with sand hills and stone buildings visible upon it.' (The buildings, some minor Maya ruins, have survived and can still be visited: **Yamil Lu'um**, next to the Sheraton, and **El Rey**, near the Club Med.) During the next 130 years, little changed around the fishing village of Puerto Juárez and what was then the backwater territory of Quintana Roo. All was not totally calm, however. In the mid-1800s Mayan Indians who had escaped the slaughter of the War of the Castes sought refuge in the impenetrable scrub jungle, where they held out for generations.

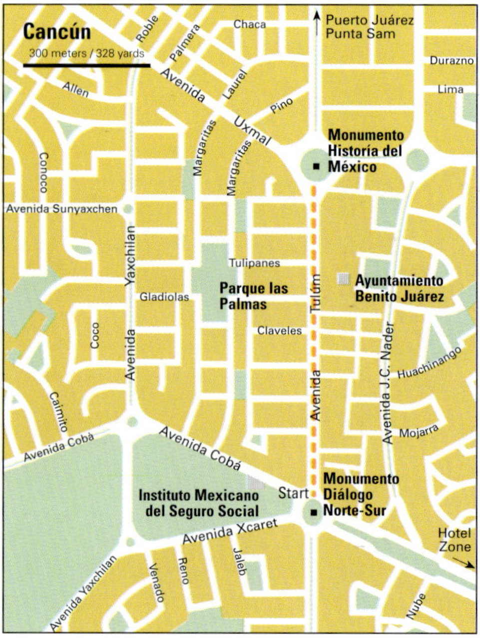

Finally, during the administration of President Luis Echeverría (1968–76), construction was begun in Cancún after a now famous computer study determined this narrow sandstrip, enclosing a brackish lagoon on the Yucatán Peninsula, to be Mexico's best site for creating a new world-class

The beach at Cancún

sea resort to rival Acapulco on the Pacific Coast. Unlike that famous port, with its extensive poor areas considered an 'eyesore' for tourists, Cancún could be created from scratch and the new town that resulted is thus fully modern, housing all levels of townspeople from hotel managers to maids and gardeners. The population, most of which services tourism, is now around 350,000. The first hotels opened in 1972 and the building boom has continued non-stop ever since.

We begin our exploration here at the heart of downtown Cancún, the hotel zone's budget neighbor. For getting around, you can take a tour (ask at your hotel or call Ceiba Tours, tel: 84-19-62 or 84-20-62), rent a car, take a taxi, go by local bus (look for those with signs saying *Hoteles* or *Turismo*) or set out on foot.

The business section, bisected by the north-south **Avenida Tulúm**, is concentrated in the area between two traffic circles. The circle at the edge of the island hotel zone is adorned with a metallic sculpture entitled *Monumento Diálogo Norte-Sur* (North-South Dialogue Monument). This commemorates a meeting of North and South American presidents during the years of President Luis Echevería's administration. At the northern end of Avenida Tulúm is the soaring *Monumento Historia del México* (History of Mexico Monument), Mexicans being proud of the fact that they have inherited cultural traditions dating back millennia.

To the west of the North-South monument is the IMSS hospital, a social security facility that provides free care to a large proportion of urban working people. Heading south on the hospital side of the *avenida*, you'll see a string of restaurants, including La Posta for Mexican food, Mr Papas for hamburgers, and Carlos O'Brian's, the downtown branch of a national chain. If you need anything from a supermarket, stop off at the incongruously named San Francisco de Asís. A modern arched building houses the Ayuntamiento

A mariachi band backed by novices

Benito Juárez, the city government offices. You can exchange money at Cunex, Tulúm 13, or at Mon Cambio Divisas, Uxmal 2, both *casas de cambio,* listing the daily rate of foreign currencies. For regular banking operations, most major Mexican banks have branches on Av Tulúm. Looking for books, newspapers, music? Fama, at Tulúm 105 near Tulipanes Street, handles publications in several languages, as does Librería Don Quixote, at Uxmal 18 near Margaritas.

A drive along the modern **hotel zone** is not to be missed, even if you're not staying there, just to see what can be achieved when a nation creates, in less than two decades, a resort with almost 20,000 hotel rooms. Virtually every current architectural concept of high-rise luxury can be found among the 50 or so establishments lining the 23-km (14-mile) long hotel row. You can enjoy the verdant lobby of the Meliá Cancún (tiers of leafy tendrils drift over the balconies) or the Parisian/London urban ambiance of the Ritz Carlton and everything between. There are a number of buildings clearly inspired by the sloping walls of Maya pyramids as well as domed colonial-style complexes.

Along **Boulevard Kukulcán** (the Mayan name for the god Quetzalcoatl), past the feathered serpent fountain, you pass an urban concentration of hotels, shopping centers and marinas. Drive all the way to the **Club Med** turnoff, which marks the end of the hotel zone, picking out the places you want to stop and see at close hand later on. You'll notice there are no street numbers along this stretch but rather indicators of the approximate distance in kilometers, for example Km 5.5. On your return, you might like to check out one or another of the shopping malls, which stock just about everything, from silver to cigars: **Plaza Caracol** has approximately 200 shops, restaurants and cafés; upscale **Plaza Kukulcán**, which is adorned with a Mayan-inspired frieze, is Cancún's newest mall offering 350 possibilities for buying; for good quality Mexican arts and crafts, check out **Plaza La Fiesta** and **Plaza Mayfair**; for shopping in a setting with a Mayan flavor, go to **Plaza Flamingo**.

One essential stop is a tour of the impressive **Centro de Convenciones** whose museum exhibits Mayan artifacts and even deformed human skulls. Most of us settle for hairdos, beards and mustaches to create distinctive head designs, but the ancient Maya favored reshaping the cranium, tattooing their flesh, and wearing stone inlays in their teeth, to name just a few of the common beautifying practices.

Among the hundreds of choices open to you for lunch, consider Cuban sandwiches at **La Cabaña**, Tulúm 21, or health food at **100% Natural**, Av Sunyaxchen 6, just across from the Hotel Caribe Internacional, which also has branches in the Terramar and Kukulcán malls and across from Expo Cancún at Av Cobá a La Luna.

Tropical fruits

After lunch, if you don't fancy an afternoon sunning on the beach, take the two-hour tour on the **Nautibus** boat, whose glass-bottomed keel offers fabulous views of fish swimming among the coral. There are two morning and two afternoon departures from Playa Tortuga Dock in the hotel zone next to Fat Tuesday restaurant (for information and reservations call 83-35-52 or 83-21-19, or check with the travel agency in your hotel).

The sea is Cancún's *raison d'être* and, although surfing is out, there are enough watersports and activities to fill your stay *(see Practical Information.)* The waters are generally calm but appearances can be deceiving – there is sometimes an invisible undertow – and you should take the usual precautions when bathing. Swim only where there's a lifeguard and observe the flags which report on swimming conditions: white for okay, green for good and black or red for dangerous. Check with the hotel staff for an explanation of the color code used.

Here is a run-down of the water sports on offer:

Diving, snorkeling and scuba: The city's many marinas offer snorkeling and scuba excursions: try **Royal Yacht Club,** across from the Omni hotel (tel: 85-03-91) and **Mundo Marino**, Blvd Kukulcán Km 5.5 (tel: 83-05-54; www.mmarino@cancun.com.mx). For the more advanced, the **Belize barrier reef**, the second longest in the world (250km/155 miles), begins near the Club Med at Punta Nizuc. As all beaches are open to the public in Cancún, including those in the hotel zone, you could head here to enjoy the clear shallow water. Cancún is not the most scenic diving spot on the peninsula –

Windsurfing: good for beginners

Jet-skiing for two

Cozumel has that honor – but you can still enjoy yourself. **Isla Mujeres** is a favorite nearby diving destination – **Scuba Cancún**, Blvd Kukulcán Km 5 (tel: 83-10-11), offers certification courses. In the event of a diving emergency, there's a decompression chamber at Total Assist Hospital, Claveles 5, downtown (tel: 87-16-88). Keen divers should pick up a copy of the magazine *Dive Mexico* for an overview of diving sites along the Caribbean coast.

Jet-skiing, water-skiing, windsurfing: **Aqua Tours**, Blvd Kukulcán Km 6.25, in front of the Dos Playas hotel (tel: 83-11-37, www.aquatours.com.mx) and **Royal Yacht Club** *(see above)* offer a full range of options, plus several other watersports.

Fishing: **Aqua Tours** and **Royal Yacht Club** offer sport fishing trips, including charters. They will arrange licenses – running from as little as three days to a full year – on your behalf.

Boat trips: Crucero Tropical (tel: 83-14-88), has daytime cruises to Isla Mujeres and a lobster dinner cruise on the *Columbus* with open bar and dancing. Boats depart from the Royal Mayan Yacht Club.

Golf: Golfers can play the 18-hole **Pok-Ta-Pok** course, (Paseo Kukulcán Km 6.5 (tel: 83-08-71) designed by Robert Trent Jones, Sr. or the 18-hole championship course at the **Caesar Park Cancún** (tel: 81-80-00). There are also championship courses at Playacar and **Puerto Aventuras** on the Cancún–Tulúm Corridor.

2. Tulúm and Cobá

A day's excursion to two very contrasting archeological sites – the sun-bleached stones of Tulúm by the sea, and Cobá, a mostly unexcavated city in the jungle. *See map on pages 18/19.*

– For Tulúm, wear sunscreen, sunglasses and a hat; and for Cobá, apply insect repellent and don long sleeves, trousers, and sturdy shoes, since you may come across snakes. –

The **Tulúm** archeological site can be reached via Highway 307, heading south from Cancún along the coast of what has come to be known as the Cancún-Tulúm Corridor. The 131km (81 miles) from Cancún can be covered in a pleasant two-hour drive. If you're already in the coastal area near Cozumel, perhaps at Xel-Há, the closest point to the ruins, you're only 13km (8 miles) away.

Tulúm, meaning 'wall', is an appropriate name for what was one of the few enclosed settlements the Maya built and virtually the only one with such an extensive boundary still standing. Visiting a then totally overgrown 'Tuloom' in the 1840s, accompanied by Frederick Catherwood who drew the buildings, John Stephens described 'the wildest scenery we had yet found in Yucatán. Besides the deep and exciting interest of the ruins themselves, we had around

View of Tulúm

us what we wanted at all the other places, the magnificence of nature. Clearing away the platform in front, we looked over an immense forest; walking around the molding of the wall, we looked out upon the boundless ocean, and deep in the clear water at the foot of the cliff we saw gliding quietly by a great fish eight or ten feet long.'

The natural setting of Tulúm, an otherwise relatively minor and rustic archeological site set at the edge of a bluff overlooking the sea, is what draws many tourists. The heavy traffic of visitors accounts for the thick bars that limit access to the interiors of several buildings, presumably to protect the few remaining murals. Try to arrive by 9am, if you hope to avoid the crowds. Early in the day is also better for taking photos. Leave before the tour buses roar in and carry on to Cobá or withdraw to a beach. You can then return before the 4pm closing to take a second look around.

As for what is known about Tulúm, it probably postdates 900AD, when the main Mayan ceremonial/urban centers were abandoned. By this time political control had weakened and the people, long past the glorious era when Mayan culture was at its height, were subject to social unrest and infighting. It was a condition reminiscent of Europe after the fall of the Roman empire, when those who could retreated behind castle walls. It may explain the rather crude masonry and artwork of Tulúm, compared to the sites that were constructed during Classic times.

Tulúm was a sort of provincial outpost, believed by some scholars to have been a fortress protecting sea trade routes, one of a series

Tulúm stands on a rugged bluff

of coastal strongholds. Sir J Eric Thompson, the renowned Mayan archeologist, regarded it as a port that channeled goods inland. A recent theory is that the tallest building, El Castillo (the Castle), was actually a lighthouse. Michael Creamer, funded by the National Geographic Society to study its function, came to the conclusion that it was a navigational station: 'We placed a lantern on shelves behind each of two windows located high on the face of the Castillo. At sea where the two beams can be seen at the same time, there's a natural opening in the reef.' If this is so, then it was still a functioning beacon when the Spanish arrived, since some conquistadors wrote that they could clearly see the light of a flame coming from the building as they sailed by.

Tulúm also has a beach

When Stephens and his companions hung their hammocks in the Castillo in the 19th century, the 6.5-hectare (16-acre) site had long been abandoned (although it may have seen some active use as a site of the Talking Cross cult from the mid-1800s into the 20th century.) Prior to the Spanish Conquest, it is estimated to have had a population of around 600 at its height, the priestly and noble classes perhaps residing inside the walls with the rest of the population huddled outside.

The **wall** itself has five entrances and the remains of what may have been watchtowers. The **Temple of Frescoes**, located just past the first buildings you see upon entering the site, is a two-story structure with columns on the bottom level and a much smaller room on top. Look between the columns to see a painting full of human figures in the style of the distant highlands and probably due to Toltec influence after they took over Chichén-Itzá. Imagine Tulúm when all the buildings were similarly sheathed in stucco and brightly painted. Note the masks extending around the corners of the facade, perhaps representing the rain god Chaac.

The two larger structures to the left were palaces. Heading towards the Castillo, you enter the heart of the walled-in ceremonial center. The platform directly in front was used as a stage for ceremonial dances – if you travel to other pre-Columbian sites, you'll see them everywhere. To the left is the **Temple of the Descending God**, which has a relief of this deity in a relatively good state of preservation over the barred door. He may have represented the Mayan bee god Ab Muxen Cab. Now ascend the steps of the **Castillo**, the most imposing building and the tallest in the complex, having been superimposed over two previous pyramids, as was common practice;

part of the roofs of these temples are visible on the right side. Note the primitive, almost naïve work of the plumed serpent columns and the corner masks.

If the Castillo functioned as a lighthouse, it would explain why there was no large window – with narrow bays it would have been easier to keep the flames burning in windy conditions. John Stephens bemoaned the fact that he and his companion couldn't enjoy a sea-view because there were only two slit-like breaks in the wall, but, he wrote, '[night] wrought a great change in our feelings. An easterly storm came on, and the rain beat heavily against the sea wall. We were obliged to stop up the oblong openings, and congratulated ourselves upon the wisdom of the ancient builders. The darkness, the howling of the winds, the cracking of branches in the forest, and the dashing of angry waves against the cliff, gave a romantic interest, almost a sublimity to our occupation of this desolate building, but we were rather too hackneyed travelers to enjoy it, and were much annoyed by moschetoes [mosquitos].'

With luck, the crowds at Tulúm won't have made you feel too 'hackneyed' to continue on to **Cobá**, but do prepare for the 'moschetoes' with insect repellent. Set around lakes a mere 40-km (25-mile) drive from Tulúm, very little of the site has been excavated. The walk on jungle paths is filled with the sound of tropical birds and the sight of delicate butterflies. Mosquitoes are a fact to be contended with in this type of terrain, so take a tip from Frederick Catherwood, who traveled with Stephens, producing invaluable illustrations of each site. Drawing at Tulúm, then as overgrown as Cobá, he was observed by Stephens: 'Looking down on him from the door of the Castillo, nothing could be finer than his position, the picturesque effect being greatly heightened by his manner of keeping one hand in his pocket, to save it from the attack of moschetoes, and by his expedient of tying his pantaloons around his legs to keep ants and other insects from running up.' Today, as we whiz from one archeological site to another in air-conditioned comfort, the hardiness of these early explorers strikes us as even more admirable.

Cobá means 'water stirred by the wind' and what a sight it must have been in its days of glory, not to mention how powerful too, as it was the hub of the Mayan highway system of

Iglesia pyramid, Cobá

no less than 50 *sacbeob*, roads even the Romans wouldn't have disdained. The longest *sacbeob*, extending over 97km (60 miles) straight through the jungle and swamplands to Yaxuná near Chichén-Itzá, was said by the archeologist Eric Thompson to average 10m (32ft) in width. 'For the greater part of its length,' wrote Thompson, one of the first to map Cobá in the 1920s, 'it is a little over two feet high, but in crossing swampy depressions, its height increases, in one case slightly more than eight feet. Walls of roughly dressed stones form the sides; large boulders topped with smaller stones laid in cement compose the bed, and the surface, now badly disintegrated, was of cement and stucco.'

This road was wider than the Great Wall of China, which was designed to permit several horsemen to ride abreast. But there were no horses in the Americas at this time. Perhaps it was because of the very lack of beasts of burden – which meant that huge numbers of people were required to transport goods between cities, especially in the absence of wheeled carts – that the roads were so wide. As the armies traveled on foot, they too took up a lot of space when on the move. Studies in the future may even indicate some astrological significance to these radiating roads.

You won't be using any *sacbeob* today but rather footpaths through the jungle. The dense vegetation cuts off the view from one group of buildings to another. The paths are marked but distances can be long – about 2km (1 mile) between the two main groupings of Cobá and Nohoch Mul, for example – so take a map and be alert. Over 6,000 structures, extending over an estimated 77sq km (30sq miles), have been identified in Cobá, although few have been restored.

Near the entrance, between lakes Cobá and Macanxoc, is the group dominated by the 24-m (80-ft) **Iglesia pyramid**, its nine terraces with rounded corners topped by a Toltec-looking temple. Depending on your stamina, you might want to climb to the top for a view or wait until you reach the Nohoch Mul group, which has the tallest pyramid in the entire northern region of the Yucatán Peninsula. On the basis of the soaring heights of the pyramids here, their narrow proportions and architectural detail, there is scholarly conjecture that Cobá traded extensively with such cities as Tikal in Guatemala, whose pyramids resemble the

Nohoch Mul

Villa Arqueológica Cobá

ones at Cobá. The elevated temples, though, are quite different, with a low, flat profile like the one on El Castillo at Chichén-Itzá (those at Tikal are topped with high sculptured crests adorning and enhancing them like the tall tortoise shell combs used by Spanish women in national dress). It's possible also that the building was abandoned before the crests were added. Cobá was settled for an unusually long time from the pre-Classic to the post-Classic era – perhaps a thousand years – probably because its location around lakes provided water, which was so difficult to come by elsewhere.

The Nohoch Mul group, 2.4km (1½ miles) east on the path, is where you'll find the 12-story **El Castillo pyramid**, which you can ascend for a fine view of the lakes, pyramids and temples poking through the treetops like so many islands in a woody green sea.

After this jungle excursion to view a formerly 'lost city' you may enjoy the contrast of a totally urbane setting for lunch at the **Villa Arqueológica Cobá**, another member of the Club Med chain that you'll find at most of Yucatán's archeological sites. Although a bit pricey, it is worth it. Go past the ticket booth, on the road along Lake Cobá and there it is, an oasis of civilization, complete with library.

3. The Cancún–Tulúm Corridor

A summary of the attractions to be found along the coastline stretching south of Cancún. This is not intended to be a timed tour, but rather a range of options, suited to a variety of tastes. Accommodation is suggested. *See map on pages 18/19.*

The portion of the Mexican Caribbean coastline designated the Cancún–Tulúm Corridor extends for around 120km (75 miles) on Highway 307. Although more of this magnificent stretch of turquoise sea and white sand beaches is being developed every day, in some areas the architects have designed the buildings to fit into the natural setting, not vice versa as was done in Cancún. Needless to say, some of the hotels are astronomically expensive, but some adventurers merely pitch a tent beside the sea. You can still find unspoiled beaches along the way, although as the bus service is erratic it is almost mandatory to have a car for successful exploration of the area. Hitchhiking is another possibility.

First stop, about 32km (20 miles) south of Cancún and 2km (1 mile) past the turnoff to the Palancar Aquarium, is the tiny fishing port of **Puerto Morelos**, from which the car ferry runs across to Cozumel. There's good scuba diving here, some hotels and a gas station – be sure to fill up as

Puerto Morelos

Snorkel in clear seas

opportunities aren't very plentiful. The expensive Caribbean Reef Club on the beach and the more moderate Hotel Playa Ojo de Agua, on Calle Javier Rojo Gómez, four blocks from the Zócalo, offer comfortable accommodation.

Another 32km (20 miles) south comes the turnoff to **Punta Bete**, on the beach at the end of a 5-km (3-mile) dirt road through a jungle of banana trees. You can string a hammock here or opt for plusher surroundings a couple of kilometers away at Las Palapas, Posada del Capitán Lafitte, or Shangri-La Caribe, with the option of thatched-roof lodgings for getting back to nature in an idyllic setting.

At **Playa del Carmen**, with its sidewalk cafés and still unspoiled atmosphere, the passenger ferry leaves for Cozumel. The town is getting more attention all the time from tourists looking for a modest, laid-back destination; there's nothing modest, however, about the Hotel Continental Plaza Playacar, set on more than 121 hectares (300 acres), with condos and villa rooms. For agreeable budget lodgings, try the Alejari. From time to time cruise ships dock here and flood the town with a temporary influx of new visitors.

Not far away is **Xcaret**, an expensive eco-archeological park (www.xcaretcancun.com.mx) whose buildings blend with the landscape. Attractions include an underground river ride, swimming with dolphins (for a hefty added fee), snorkeling, swimming, a botanical garden, museum, aquarium and wild bird sanctuary. A dinner show includes a display of traditional dance by the Flying Indians of Papantla.

The offshore coral reef here has become a mecca for scuba divers who enjoy exploring the remains of a Spanish galleon that sunk

Seaside dining at Xcacel

here in the 18th century. Some of the objects retrieved from the wreck, along with an exhibit on the history of diving in the area from the times of the ancient Maya, can be seen in the CEDAM museum in **Puerto Aventuras**, an upmarket resort with a 300-berth marina, a golf course and other luxurious amenities.

Akumal, meaning 'Place of the Turtles,' because of the many sea turtles that come here to lay their eggs, is another eco-tourism destination, with a very large beach, upscale hotels and bungalows. The highway arrived here only about 30 years ago, financed by developers who constructed luxury hotels and bungalows along a fine stretch of palm-lined beach. The moderately expensive Hotel Club Akumal Caribe provides a variety of lodgings, a dive shop and a range of special summer packages (tel: 1-800-351-1622, in the US; 1-800-343-1440, in Canada). **Xcacel Beach**, 119km (74 miles) from Cancún, is sublime. Backing on to a charming palm grove where a discreet campsite nestles, it offers solitary walks along the shore, outdoor eating in a *palapa* (thatched-roof) restaurant or lazing in brightly colored locally woven hammocks.

Xel-Há, 110km (70 miles) from Cancún, is a national park (www. xel-ha.com.mx) comprising lagoons of transparent waters filled with kaleidoscopic marine life. Try not to wear sunscreen, which washes off and poisons the wildlife (it's best to wear a T-shirt to protect against the sun while swimming). Xel-Há has several small Mayan ruins, along with restaurants and gift shops.

Sian Ka'an Biosphere Reserve

At **Dos Ojos**, about 1km (½ mile) inland from Xel-Há, you can cave dive with scuba equipment or snorkel (with no gear at all in one dry cave). Local Indians are participants in running this site in the jungle.

South of Tulúm *(see Itinerary 2)* is the enormous *Reserva de la Biósfera Sian Ka'an* (Sian Ka'an Biosphere Reserve), one of UNESCO's World Network of Biosphere Reserves. For over a decade its organizers have been seeking to save this region from overdevelopment, while providing a living for the local people through ecological farming methods. A system of ancient Mayan canals and a score of archeological sites have been discovered on the land. The reserve also protects hundreds of species of animal life. A guided tour in the company of a biologist is available through Los Amigos del Sian Ka'an in Cancún (tel: 84-95-83) if you get yourself to Boca Paila or Cabañas Ana y José, in Tulúm. Ecocolors has tours to Sian Ka'an leaving from Cancún on specific weekdays.

4. Isla Mujeres and Cozumel

A trip from Cancún to Isla Mujeres or Cozumel.

These two islands off the Mexican Caribbean coast are very different from each other: Isla Mujeres is quite small, navigable on foot by intrepid walkers and still somewhat relaxed, at least compared to neighboring, high-rise Cancún. Cozumel, down the coast, is totally flat and liberally sprinkled with Mayan ruins. It is the nation's diving Mecca, with Palancar one of the longest coral reefs in the world.

Isla Mujeres

On a map **Isla Mujeres** looks rather like a diving fish – at its snout is one of its two lighthouses and the ruins of a Mayan temple, the fin on its belly encloses the Laguna Makax, a hollow in the middle encloses a long narrow pond called Salina Grande, and its tail is the site of the town. Two roads run from one end to the other of the 8-km (5-mile) long island, which is just 0.5km (¼ mile) wide in many places and narrows to even less than this in others. Located a mere 13km (8 miles) from Cancún, Isla Mujeres is a world away in atmosphere. It is laid-back and relaxed.

Docked at Isla Mujeres

Boats to the island depart from Cancún from three different points: **Puerto Juárez**, a few kilometers north of downtown Cancún, offers a passenger boat service almost hourly for less than $3 US; **Playa Linda pier** in the hotel zone, next to the Hotel Casa Maya, offers a catamaran service; and **Punta Sam**, 5km (3 miles) south of Puerto Juárez, offers a car ferry. Asterix has a water taxi service that leaves Club Nautica/Playa Caracol four times daily (US $13.50 round trip).

Isla Mujeres, which means Island of Women, sounds like a fantasy but there are at least two explanations for the name. One theory is that the first Spaniards who arrived noted a large number of female idols in the temples (probably in honor of Ixchel, the goddess of fertility) and dubbed the place accordingly. The more swashbuckling theory is that the pirates who roved these waters kept their women sequestered here.

Most visitors snorkel, scuba dive or just laze on a beach. The first thing to do when you arrive, if you plan to stay overnight or longer, is to secure a hotel room: there is a choice of over 20 hotels in the small town *(see Practical Information)*, all of which are modest compared with the accommodations in Cancún's hotel zone. After getting settled, a 15-minute walk around the town will cover

Rent a bike on Isla Mujeres

the main sights and also uncover some promising-looking eateries for later. If you're ready for the beach, take Guerrero, Hidalgo or Carlos Lazo streets toward Coco beach (**Playa Cocoteros**) located at the nearby northern end of the island, where the water is shallow and calm but likely to be packed with other sunseekers.

Exploring other parts of the island will probably be more fun – you can hire a taxi for a few dollars or rent a bicycle or motorbike at one of the many stands (make sure the motorbike's gas tank is full); alternatively rent a moped or electric golf cart at P'pes at Av Hidalgo 19 (tel: 7-00-19), take a local bus, or hike. In all cases take sun protection, and if you plan to return by ferry in the afternoon, make sure you don't miss the boat.

For our island tour, we take **Avenida Gustavo Rueda Medina**, heading in a southerly direction past the small airport, then between the Salina Grande pond and the Laguna Makax. Straight ahead are a series of beaches (Playa Pescador, Playa Lancheros and Playa Indios) but the most attractive is a little farther on – **Playa Garrafón**. This is in a national park and offers beach amenities such as chairs, lockers, snorkeling equipment for hire, and also a modest place to eat.

If land exploring is more to your taste, check out the nearby lighthouse, as well as the ruins of what may have been a Mayan lighthouse-cum-temple. Also close at hand is the **Hacienda Mundaca** (also called a fort) of which very little remains.

Play on the 'playa'

Its legend is that Spanish pirate Fermín Antonio Mundaca fell in love with a beautiful woman on Isla Mujeres and built a magnificent house to win her heart but she disdained him, married somebody else, and left the pirate bereft. Then, depending on which version of the story you read, he either died of a broken heart or lived out his lonely days here, leaving the house to fall into ruin.

To explore the wilder side of the island, head back north on the road on the Caribbean side, where you'll follow an undeveloped coastline. For lunch, you might like to try the pricey but excellent cuisine of María's Kan Kin Restaurant Française, near **Garrafón beach**, where you'll eat under the thatched roof of a *palapa* in a setting of casual elegance. Or you might want to save a leisurely meal for the evening and just grab a quick bite at Garrafón or head back to town for a choice of possibilities.

Nature-lovers who plan to stay on the island for a few days may enjoy a one- or two-day trip to **Isla Contoy**, a bird sanctuary where scores of species thrive. Located about two hours away by boat, a one-day tour includes landing on the island, walking up to the top of the observation tower for a sweeping view of the bird life, a swim with snorkel equipment and all meals, one of which is freshly caught fish cooked over an open fire on the beach. Check at your hotel or at the **Sociedad Cooperativa Transporte Turística** on Av Rueda Medina, next to the Mexico Divers office. This is a boatmen's cooperative which arranges fishing trips. Take a look at the boats first, as some have canopies for sun protection and others do not.

Cozumel

You can reach Cozumel directly from Cancún via a 15-minute shuttle flight on Mexicana's Aerocozumel (tel: 84-20-00 in Cancún); take a leisurely scenic drive down the coast to Playa del Carmen in under 1½ hours; or go by bus in less than an hour. There are two types of passenger ferry service to Cozumel from the dock near the main plaza in Playa del Carmen. For those who tend to get seasick easily, the recommended choice is the *MV Mexico* waterjet, a fully enclosed, air-conditioned vessel with comfortable airplane seats. It hovers above the sea, thus avoiding rough water movements and arrives in 30 minutes. More traditional service is available in the *Xel-Há* (among other vessels), where the open air and movement of the sea are pleasant experiences in themselves for good sailors, at half the cost and twice the traveling time.

Schedules are irregular but there are several departures daily. Try to have the exact change to avoid hassles with ticket-sellers who often run out of coins.

Hop on a boat for Cozumel

Taking shade

Those who want to take their car to Cozumel, must drive to **Puerto Morelos**, about 16km (10 miles) south of Cancún, where they may have to wait in a line of vehicles for a couple of hours. All passenger ferries to Cozumel arrive in downtown San Miguel on Av Melgar and Benito Juárez Street, while car ferries and cruise ships arrive at the wharf farther south.

Unlike Cancún, which was virtually developed from scratch, **San Miguel** is an established town that was once based on fishing. The island itself has had peaks and valleys of human activity and habitation, reaching one particular high point after the fall of the mainland Mayan cities after 900AD, when it was an important trading center, as well as a religious center of the goddess Ixchel. Women would travel here seeking her divine intervention in matters of love and fertility. Cozumel must have seen much more intense boat traffic at that time than today, as evidenced by the 10 sites of Mayan ruins, which may have been places of pilgrimage.

After the arrival of the Spanish, the population was decimated by disease and by the 19th century the island had become almost uninhabited, only being re-colonized by Indians from the Talking Cross sect after the mid-century War of the Castes. Little by little the population grew, partially because of the world demand for chewing-gum, the raw material of which was harvested from local trees. When Jacques Cousteau filmed here in the early 1960s, drawing attention to the incredible beauty of Palancar reef, the stage was set for eventual tourist development, but it wasn't until Cancún's spectacular rise that Cozumel became a major destination.

Present-day visitors can enjoy the calm pace of San Miguel, where budget and mid-price lodgings are available, or opt for more luxury in the hotels north and south of town. Divers have available to them a choice of more than a dozen dive shops for equipment in town and several reefs for memorable submarine explorations. Development has been concentrated on the western shore, with the east coast left practically virgin and taking the full force of normal seawinds, as well as tropical hurricanes.

For a one-day tour, you'll want to check out a bit of the town, being sure to visit the attractive **Museo de la Isla de Cozumel** on the seafront, Av Rafael Melgar, just a couple of blocks north of the ferry dock at Calle Benito Juárez. Housed in an attractive old building, the well-designed exhibits provide full coverage of the island's history, both natural and cultural, explaining, for instance, how coral is formed and illustrating the local flora and fauna. Upstairs are pieces from both the pre-Hispanic and Spanish colonial era. A pleasant second floor terrace café offers ocean views.

For getting around, you can take a package tour (the more expensive of which include snorkeling and a meal); rent a car or motorbike or go by taxi, which for a complete tour will cost around the same price as a car rental ($50). Head south on Av Melgar, past some upscale hotels, to **Laguna Chankanaab Parque Nacional**, less than 10km (6 miles) from San Miguel. Its beautiful setting of white beaches, dense vegetation, crystal-clear lagoon (now off-limits to swimmers) and *palapas* is indeed a tropical paradise and probably what you've traveled so far to enjoy. It has all the comforts of restrooms, eateries and diving equipment for rent. Walk around to enjoy the reproduction Mayan buildings set in a botanical garden and observe the marine life in the lagoon.

Afterwards, continue south, past the reefs that make Cozumel an international diving destination (Yocaab, Santa Rosa, Palancar, Colombia and Maracaibo), skirting the southern tip where both the Celarain lighthouse and Caracol ruins stand, and then head north through the dramatic landscapes of the east coast. Stop to walk along the beaches and look for shells. Swimming is not recommended because of the dangerous undertow, although **Punta Chiqueros** and **Punta Morena** are considered safer.

The road veers left at Santa Cecilia and you may enjoy taking a look at the partially restored **San Gervasio** ruins; a couple of kilometers ahead you'll see the right-hand turnoff to the site, which is about 8km (5 miles) farther on. Refresh yourself with a cold drink at the snack stand before continuing west back to town.

Celarain Point

Chichén-Itzá

5. Chichén-Itzá

A tour of Chichén-Itzá, the capital of the Toltec empire. If you are traveling to Chichén-Itzá from Cancún, break your journey at Valladolid *(see Itinerary 6)*.

Avoid the one-day tours to **Chichén-Itzá** from Cancún if at all possible, since most of your time will be spent on the road and you'll be rushed around this sprawling archeological site at the hottest and most crowded time of day. There are several hotels within walking distance of the 10-sq km (4-sq mile) site: the **Hotel Mayaland**, only around 152m (500ft) from the eastern entrance (near the Observatory), is the oldest and most gracious of them.

El Castillo

At the main entrance, check out the pleasant visitors' center, with its bookstore, restaurant, small museum and clean restrooms. Once in the grounds of the site, note that north is to your left. The ruins in the northern section are from a later date and show the influence of the highland Toltec culture that came from the vicinity of present-day Mexico City to occupy the city around 900AD. The southern section is older and most buildings are in the Puuc style, seen in such other sites as Uxmal.

The structure that dominates Chichén-Itzá is the pyramid the Spaniards called **El Castillo**, as they dubbed so many of the pyramid temples they found. It is more accurately the Temple to Kukulcán, one of the most important Mayan deities, whose cult was brought here by the invading Toltecs (who called him Quetzalcoatl). This god is represented graphically as a plumed serpent and this symbol decorates the balustrade of the staircases on each of the four sides of the pyramid. The flat-roofed temple on top is Toltec.

In the Ball Court

The pyramid incorporates key time measurements in its structure: its four staircases have 91 steps each and, including the platform at the top as one step, the total number is therefore 365, the number of days in a year. Each side has 52 panels (the design looks like square scallops), representing the 52-year cosmic cycle, the point at which the two calendars, the religious and the secular, coincided and when they considered that time ended, only to begin anew.

At the spring equinox (March 21) thousands come to Chichén-Itzá to witness a memorable event: the play of sunlight on the balustrade of the northern staircase gives the appearance of a living serpent that is creeping down towards the head at the foot of the pyramid to slither into the ground. Mayan priests claimed this phenomenon was Kukulcán's signal that the time for sowing crops had arrived. In contrast, at the fall equinox (September 21) the snake appears to ascend, indicating that the crops should be harvested. This effect was an astonishing feat of the original architects, as most archeological sites in the world are oriented so that the sun merely strikes a strategic spot at some time during the year, while here the light and shadows create the illusion of a living being – a moving picture-show long before electricity.

Here, as in other places in Mesoamerica, pyramid was built over pyramid, covering up the old structure in what some scholars believe to have been the 52-year time cycle. You can see the overlap for yourself when you go beneath the present structure and ascend

Temple of the Warriors

the staircase of the pyramid underneath. You'll reach a niche with an altar in the form of a rustic sculpture of a red jaguar, encrusted with green stones. There is also a Chac Mool sculpture. The limited times this area is open are listed beside the entrance. Caution: this exercise is not for claustrophobics.

The evidence of Toltec residence here is most palpable at the **Temple of the Warriors** and **the Thousand Columns**, which stand to the right of the main pyramid, when you are facing north. If you compare your view of this section to photos of Tula, you'll notice an astonishing resemblance. Archeologists and anthropologists are now enjoying a new debate – since the temple complex at Tula is much more rustic than this one, could Indians from here have colonized the highlands? Or, more likely, the Toltecs recreated their hometown using the labor of the Maya, who had a much higher level of craftsmanship. The pyramid is much lower than is usual in Yucatán and the larger platform at the top meant that a roomier temple could be built. The feathered serpent pillars at the entrance plus the interior columns may have been topped by wooden beams to support a roof.

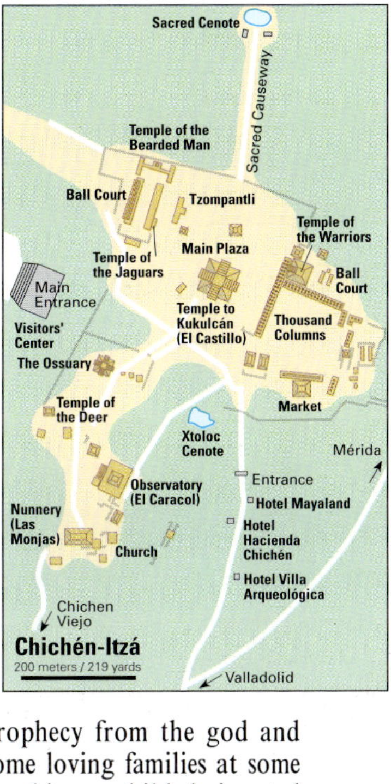

Now, head away from this section, with the pyramid behind you and the Temple of the Warriors to your right, to visit the waters of the sacred *cenote*. These natural sinkholes dot the landscape of the northern Yucatán lowlands and at one time were the only source of water. Some, such as this one, were used for ritual purposes – people were thrown into the holes as human sacrifices to the rain god Chaac. Some sources say that anyone still alive after a given amount of time was considered as chosen to communicate a prophecy from the god and pulled out – it's not hard to imagine some loving families at some out-of-the-way *cenote* surreptitiously teaching a child designated for sacrifice how to tread water.

The dark waters have been investigated on two occasions: the first exploration, sponsored by Harvard University's Peabody Museum, was carried out in 1903–07 by US consul Edward Thompson, who found skeletons and precious objects of jade and gold, obviously brought from a great distance, since there was none in the peninsula. Thompson nearly lost his life in some dives, but his heroic efforts were overshadowed by his secretly having the dredged-up pieces sent to the US (many have since been returned). The second exploration, when hundreds of objects were salvaged, was under the direction of the National Geographic Society in the 1960s. Before returning to the main buildings, you may want to take a break at the refreshment area (with restrooms) near the *cenote.*

Afterwards, bear right to pass by a low platform, where rows of skulls are incised in the stone. A Toltec contribution called a *tzompantli* or skull rack, this platform may have been the base for a framework used to exhibit the skulls of sacrificial victims. A similar rack to this one has been unearthed at the main temple in Mexico City.

Now, you are at one of the most intriguing structures here, the carefully restored **Ball Court**, which is the largest and best preserved anywhere in Mesoamerica. Most of the Mayan cities had ball courts and Chichén-Itzá had nine of them. The ritual game played here, in a space longer than an American football field, is still somewhat mysterious, although it's known that two teams wearing lots of padding propelled a heavy rubber ball around without using their hands or feet, bouncing it off their hips and shoulders. The rings on each side were a target for shooting the ball through – a seemingly difficult feat. For one team the result may have been fatal, for the reliefs at the end of the field seem to indicate that one team's members were decapitated: check out the headless kneeling figure with writhing snakes, symbolizing blood, coming out of his neck. Some say it was the winners who were 'honored' in this way, others that the losers had to pay the price of their defeat.

The 'skull rack'

A less grisly theory is that the winners got to keep the clothing and jewelry of the spectators. But where did the spectators sit? There's no evidence of any built-in seating. If the competition was meant to signify a cosmic event, it may be that only a handful of people attended and they sat up high in the Temple of the Jaguar, reaching their vantage point by ascending the side stairs.

For a look at the older part of the city, head south to reach the **Observatory**, called the *Caracol* (snail) because of its winding interior stairway. The Maya were assiduous observers of the heavens and the fascinating thing about this ancient structure is its resemblance to modern observatories – the main difference is that there were no telescopes here but painstaking calculations, based on exact observations made over a long period of time. This structure, which is elevated on two platforms, may be partially Toltec but the mask depicts the Mayan rain god Chaac.

The Annex of Las Monjas

Continue farther on to reach a fine example of classic Mayan architecture in the Puuc style of Uxmal, usually characterized by a plain lower wall and heavily decorated overhanging upper portions, said to represent the proportions of the thatched Mayan hut, the *na*. The first structure to observe is the small building called the **Church**, adorned by hook-nosed Chaac masks at different points, most strikingly at the corners. For a particularly florid example of this style, go up the rather crumbling stairs to visit the buildings at the top designated as **Las Monjas** (the Nunnery) by the Spanish, to the so-called Annex, which is totally covered by Chaac masks, lattice panels and moldings.

For those who want to explore caves, the **Gruta de Balancanché**, 6km (3½ miles) away, offer guided tours in different languages. The hours are posted at the entrance to Chichén-Itzá.

Staying overnight at Chichén-Itzá is advantageous because you can then visit the ruins early in the morning or late in the afternoon, avoiding the midday heat and tourist rush and spending the most uncomfortable hours of the day having a leisurely lunch, taking a siesta, reading up on the site or enjoying a cool swim. In addition to the Mayaland mentioned above, other hotels near to the site are the **Hacienda Chichén**, with its refurbished bungalows. This building belonged to Edward H Thompson, the American consul who excavated the Chichén-Itzá *cenote*, and was later the headquarters of many archeological excavation teams. Another option is the **Hotel Villa Arqueológica**, where you can enjoy a good French-Mayan table and the usual Club Med amenities.

Traditional dress

6. Valladolid

This is a good place to break a trip to or from Chichén-Itzá.

Although Valladolid is now only a sleepy provincial town, in the middle of the 19th century it had almost the same population as Mérida, before it was nearly wiped out by the Indian insurgents in the War of the Castes. It has a trio of architectural sites worth admiring: the **Catedral de San Servacio**, the **Convento de San Bernardino de Siena** and the **Palacio Municipal**.

The generally plain lines of the colonial churches and buildings in this small city are indicative of the early date it was founded – nearly 450 years ago, when the Spanish weren't in a position to expend much time on luxurious details but rather concentrated on quickly erecting substantial buildings to establish a presence and express their political and religious domination over the Indians, whose city of Zací had previously stood on this site. Valladolid is only about 40km (25 miles) from Chichén-Itzá, and some people prefer to stay overnight here because of the generally lower prices. Some possibilities are: **Hotel Mendoza**, Calle 39 (between 44 & 46) tel: 62002, and **Hotel Mesón del Marqués**, Calle 39 No 203 (tel: 62072). Both are on the main plaza. Some eating possibilities are: **Hostería del Marqués** (in the Hotel El Mesón del Marqués); **Casa de los Arcos**, Calle 39 No 200A, and **Hotel María de la Luz**, Calle 42 No 195 (tel: 62071). All serve Mexican cuisine, specializing in Yucatecan dishes and are very popular with the *Vallisoletanos* (the citizens of Valladolid).

Before leaving town, check out the **Zací** *cenote* to see a sinkhole that has a cave tucked into its steep sides – Calle 36 between Calles 37 and 39. The Dzitnup *cenote*, 4km (2½ miles) southwest of town is better for swimming. The park in the main plaza is always ready for visitors with its huge ring of park benches.

A storm brews in Valladolid

Mérida

7. Mérida

This is a full day's itinerary in Mérida. Enjoy stately Mexican colonial architecture as well as French mansions built by henequen tycoons; take a buggy ride; attend a dance fest in the evening, in a city that stages a public event every day of the week.
See map on page 44.

Where old-world atmosphere prevails

Charming, cultured Mérida now has nearly a million inhabitants. In the colonial downtown, where an old-world atmosphere prevails, horses and buggies mingle with motor traffic and every block seems to have a bookstore and at least one place to eat. People sit under the arcade by the **Zócalo** at eateries which look the same as they do in photos taken in the early 1900s, where all the patrons were men and almost everyone, including the waiters, wore a hat. Leafy patios surrounded by arcades with high ceilings and cool black and white checked tile floors abound. Inviting restaurants beckon, the diners sitting on dignified Chippendale or Empire-style chairs enjoying delicious Cuban coffee.

Once enclosed by walls, as was Campeche, the downtown area is compact, with narrow streets and closely packed buildings filling the limited space available within the fortifications. This is ideal territory for a walking tour, as many of the main sights are within a short distance of each other. Laid out on a grid plan with numbered streets (even numbers run north-south, odd numbers east-west), the Zócalo is bound by Calle 60 and Calle 62 and Calles 61 and 63. This plaza is an inviting place for a stroll, with its laurel trees that arch over the sidewalks and park benches providing welcome shade. Mérida has long been known as the White City and although no-one knows with any certainty how that description originated, several reasons have been put forward: the number of white buildings once here, the white garments worn by the townspeople, its striking cleanliness.

Mérida
300 meters / 328 yards
Parque de las Américas
Santa Isabel
Finish
Start
Museo de Antropología e Historia (Palacio Cantón)
Santa Ana
Parque de Santa Ana
Santa Lucía
Parque de Santa Lucía
Centro de Información Turística
Universidad de Yucatán
Teatro Peón Contreras
Plaza de la Maternidad
Iglesia de Tercera Orden
Biblioteca
Museo de Arte Popular
Pinacoteca del Juan Gamboa Guzmán
Palacio de Gobierno
Parque Hidalgo
Museo de la Ciudad
Escuela de Arquitectura (La Mejorada)
Ayuntamiento
Plaza de Armas
Zócalo
Catedral
Museo de la Canción Yucateca
Iglesia las Monjas
Ateneo Peninsular
Arco de Dragones
Casa de Montejo
Arco del Puente
Mercado de Artesanías
Mercado Municipal
Parque de San Juan
San Juan Bautista
Arco de San Juan
San Cristóbal
Paseo de Montejo
Calle 41
Calle 43
Calle 45
Calle 47
Calle 49
Calle 51
Calle 53
Calle 55
Calle 57
Calle 59
Calle 61
Calle 63
Calle 65
Calle 67
Calle 69
Calle 71
Calle 72
Calle 68
Calle 66
Calle 64
Calle 62
Calle 60
Calle 58
Calle 56
Calle 54
Calle 52
Calle 50
Calle 48

Mérida's cathedral

Begin at the rather stark church, the oldest mainland **cathedral** in the Americas. Compared to the extremely ornate stone facades in the highlands, so complex that they have been the subject of master's theses, this one is quite simple, although pleasing. It has the air of a fortress and may have had that function in the early days when the Conquest had yet to be consolidated. Before the coming of the Spanish, the Mayan city located here was called **T'ho**, which means the **Place of the Five Temples**. When the conquistadors finally subdued the Indians in 1542, the victors were so struck by the appearance of the temples, which reminded them of the Roman ruins in Mérida, Spain, that they named their settlement in honor of the city in their homeland. They lost no time, however, in dismantling the buildings they so admired, using the stones to erect the cathedral. It was built by Indians and just under the crosses the tall twin towers are topped by a subtle shingle effect that one local guide is convinced symbolizes the Maya god Kukulcán, the plumed serpent coiled around the highest point of the edifice, the place of honor it might have held at the summit of a pyramid.

Inside, the austere feeling continues. It lacks the golden altarpieces found in so many Mexican churches but has one of the largest crucified Christs anywhere, measuring at least 3m (10ft). The church, sacked during the 19th-century War of the Castes, has a kind of sober majesty about it with its enormous columns, round arches, coffered ceiling and dome, in keeping with the spirit of the Franciscan order. Be sure to visit the crucifix of Christ of the Blisters in a side chapel to the left of the main altar, considered miraculous for having survived a couple of fires. It is revered by Méridians, who hold an annual festival from September 28 to October 13 in its honor.

Back outside, cross Calle 60 to enter the **Palacio de Gobierno** on the corner, to admire some impressive paintings depicting the

Inside the Palacio de Gobierno

history of Yucatán. Admission is free. These brilliantly executed and powerful works by Fernando Castro Pachecho start on the stairwell, with mythical subjects, and continue in the history room upstairs. Look out for the period when the Maya were sold as slaves to Cuba after the War of the Castes.

For a total change of pace, visit the **Plaza Picheta** shopping center, to the right under the arcade, offering arts and crafts, recorded music and embroidered clothing among other things. Several modest restaurants around here have been in business for at least a century and you might like to stop for a cool drink.

Cross the street to the **Ayuntamiento** (city hall) for a quick look at a mural depicting the threat of nuclear war, before continuing to the right on Calle 63 for a stopover at the **Iglesia las Monjas** in the next block to check out the Casa de las Artesanías for well-made arts and crafts.

Returning to the Zócalo via Calle 63, head to the right side to view the distinctive facade of the **Casa de Montejo**, one of the most beautiful buildings in Mexico. Built in the mid-1500s by Francisco de Montejo el Mozo, it was the home of successive generations of the Montejo family until the 1980s when it was taken over for banking offices by Banamex. The elaborate facade depicts two conquistadors symbolically standing on the heads of the defeated Indians – many Mayan stelai have similar images of a victor literally walking all over the defeated. The two smaller figures on each side, looking as if they've been tarred and feathered, apparently represent savages preparing to defend the Montejos with the clubs they're holding. Each window of the palace bears the coat of arms of a branch of the Montejo family.

Wind up this circuit of the plaza next to the cathedral at the **Ateneo Peninsular**, once the residence of the archbishop, then used by the military, and now a museum of contemporary art, **Museo Macay**. Note its triangular pediment with two fleshy Greek goddesses reclining on either side. If you'd like a peek at photographs of historical Mérida, turn right at Calle 61 to visit the **Museo de la Ciudad**, housed in the former church of San Juan de Dios at the corner of Calle 58.

To find a place for lunch, stroll along Calle 60, which runs in front of the cathedral. On your left is the **Teatro Daniel Ayala** and to the right such stores as El Alamo, for arts and crafts, and La Bohemia with its antiques. The **Parque Hidalgo**, one block ahead on the right, is lively, with courting benches in the center – 'S'-shaped seating for couples, which allow them to gaze into each other's eyes while blocking further liberties, a holdover from a different age. In the center is a statue to General Manuel Cepeda Peraza, who lived in the 19th century. The small plaza is officially named after him but the majority of people still call it Parque Hidalgo.

Pediment of the Ateneo Peninsular

Homely bar café in Mérida

Encircled by eateries with outdoor tables, check out: **Hotel Restaurant el Patio** for Spanish food; **Pizzas Giorgio** and **El Mesón**. Eat outside for people-watching or retire into the cool quiet of the **Hotel Caribe** to sample some Yucatecan specialties. A few steps farther up 60 on the left is **La Bella Epoca** upstairs in the Hotel del Parque, with tall Chippendale chairs and a menu encompassing Mexican, Arab, International and 'Naturalist' (health) food. On the corner of the plaza, **Librería Dante** stocks books on Mexico and the Yucatán in particular.

Local girls

Continue north on Calle 60, with a quick look into the **Iglesia de Tercera Orden** (Church of the Third Order) to see its painted interior. A block ahead is the intimate **Plaza de la Maternidad**, flanked on one side by the early 20th century **Teatro Peón Contreras**, where you can perhaps peep in to see a rehearsal. Check out the posters in the lobby to see what's on, as some events are free. The building also houses a Dante bookstore, an art gallery and the **Restaurant Café Peón Contreras**, pleasant to visit any time with its ceiling fans, dark wooden furniture, and mirrored bar graced by intriguing blonde, rosy-complexioned angels with kohl-rimmed eyes. Waiters in black berets serve strong Cuban coffee, as well as Yucatecan specialties, such as *camarones al ajillo* (shrimp in garlic sauce).

Just across the street is the Felipe Carrillo Puerto University Theater and a few steps ahead the main building of the **Universidad de Yucatán**. The university was refounded by 1920s governor Felipe Carrillo Puerto. Check out the bulletin board for activities.

Paseo de Montejo mansion

One block ahead at the corner of Calle 57 is the shady **Parque de Santa Lucía**, with the church of the same name which, when Mérida was still surrounded by walls, marked the northern city limits. (This neighborhood was designated for blacks and mulattoes, the downtown area was for Spaniards and the Santiago section was for Indians.) Today the park is the center of a lively cultural life. Cross over to the corner of the arcade to see the **Poets' Corner**, adorned with busts of some of the most beloved figures of Yucatán's artistic past: from left to right are Ricardo López Méndez, poet; Ricardo Palmerín, composer; Luis Rosado Vega; Cirilo Baquiero, father of Yucatecan song; Ermilio Padrón López; Guty Cárdenas, tenor; Pepe Domínguez.

There are several ways of exploring Mérida, once called the Paris of the West. In addition to walking tours such as the ones we have made, you can take a two-hour tour in a bus with old-fashioned wooden seats and a striped canvas awning from the Parque de Santa Lucía. With four daily departures (10am, 1pm, 4pm and 7pm) and a bilingual guide, **Transportadora Turística Carnaval** (tel: 27-61-19) visits 30 sights, extending from one end of town to the other. Soft drinks are for sale on board.

You can cover a lot of ground in one of the nostalgic *calesas* (horse-drawn carriages) including downtown (be careful to arrange the route and price with the driver before setting out.) In the downtown area around the cathedral, you may be approached by amateur guides, some of whom are quite well informed, and enthusiastic, about their native city. Again, come to an agreement on the price before starting off. Considering that Mérida has tropically hot weather for much of the year, it would be a good idea to visit the more distant sights by vehicle, saving those in the city center for the morning or late afternoon when the sun isn't beating down from directly overhead.

Since you're at the departure point of Carnaval tour buses, this might be the time to board, as it will comfortably transport you to other parts of the city without the hassle of looking at maps and getting lost. The bus will continue along Calle 60 to the **Parque de Santa Ana**, whose arch is one of the remaining few from colonial days.

A right on Calle 47 leads to **Paseo de Montejo**, a wide, shady boulevard created in the 19th century – Mérida's answer to Mexico City's Paseo de la Reforma and Paris's Champs Elysées. When henequen was the 'green gold' of the Yucatán, the tycoons who made their fortunes out of the crop (used for making rope) built mansions along this avenue, some of which are still standing today. It's not hard to imagine their lives of elegant luxury: their children educated at the best schools in Europe, their wives dressed in the latest Parisian finery – all attained, however, at the expense of their Indian laborers, who were practically serf-slaves. Note the identical twin palaces of the **Barbachano** family on your left.

Ahead is the famous **Palacio Cantón**, the most ornate of them all – it now houses the excellent **Museo de Antropología e Historia**, where you can get an overview of Yucatán's history, including information on the Maya.

You'll see several monuments along the way: the first being to **Felipe Carrillo Puerto**, tagged the Red Governor because of all the reforms he tried to implement in the 1920s to help the downtrodden Indians. Falling in love with American journalist Alma Reed, he left his family and openly lived with her, a tremendous social scandal at the time. One of the most famous love songs in Mexico, *La Peregrina* (The Wanderer) was written at his request and in her honor. Assassinated by his enemies while still governor, he's still remembered as a romantic figure, whose reforms were ahead of their time.

The next statue is to **Justo Sierra**, the father of Yucatán literature as well as a great educator. The bus stops at the third statue, the ostentatious **Monumento a la Patria**, about which the guide will offer a full explanation. Created more than half a century ago by Colombian sculptor Romulo Rozo, partially at his own expense, it is fashioned out of stone brought from the city of Ticul.

The circular composition portrays the history of Mexico – in the center, the fountain represents the lake where the Aztec Indians built their city of Tenochtitlán (present-day Mexico City) and the names and coats of arms of the 32 Mexican states surround it. Around the back the story begins with Maya and Aztec warriors and covers the different culminating moments that shaped the country's destiny.

Continuing along Paseo de Montejo, in the heart of modern Mérida, with its many restaurants, hotels and stores, you'll

Monumento a la Patria

Elegant inhabitant

encounter sudden flashbacks to the past such as the name of a supermarket chain called San Francisco de Asis, which is a reminder of the enduring influence of the Franciscan order on the life of the peninsula.

The tour stops off at **Parque de las Américas**, another Romulo Rozo work created between 1942 and 1945. Divided into four sections, it includes an open-air theater (the Rozo mural around the stage depicts Mayan fine arts), now used for children's festivals; a playground, a striking fountain and library, all with beautifully conceived and executed pre-Hispanic motifs.

Among the other sights covered on the tour is the **Santiago Park**, located in what was an Indian neighborhood in colonial times, with another of the few remaining city entrance arches. A small church, the **Ermita de Santa Isabel**, traditionally visited by travelers before they set out on the Royal Road to Campeche, sits beside a cool and interesting botanical garden.

To cover Mérida and the surrounding area thoroughly, you'll need several days to spare. In keeping with Mérida's cultured image, an astonishing variety of free (or almost free) cultural events – Mariachi bands, concerts, dance performances, rodeos – are offered almost daily by the city (usually at 8 or 9pm), with a special event series 'Mérida en Domingo' on Sundays. *(See the Nightlife section for more details.)*

Hire a horse-drawn carriage on the Plaza de la Maternidad

8. Uxmal and Kabáh

A full-day excursion from Mérida to the archeological sites of Uxmal and Kabáh. For those who love archeological sites and great architecture, this will be one of the high points of their visit to the Yucatán. *See map of Uxmal on page 53.*

– If you are driving, take Highway 261 heading south out of Mérida for around 72km (45 miles) to reach the site, or leave the driving to others and take a guided tour. –

The name **Uxmal** means thrice-built or thrice-occupied place and, besides being one of the most beautiful archeological sites anywhere in the world, Uxmal is the zenith of the Puuc or hill style of Mayan architecture. If your time is limited, this is one of the two sites you should see in the Yucatán, the other being Chichén-Itzá. The Uxmal builders created an urban *tour de force*, designing a purely Mayan city uninfluenced by outsiders. It wasn't created all at once but added to over time, which perhaps explains its name.

Entry to the site is via the **Visitors' Center**, a compact complex of stores, restaurant, museum and clean restrooms built around a pleasant central patio. You may find a meal and/or drink here very inviting after visiting the ruins. Uxmal can be divided into three groupings of buildings, which are located in relation to the entrance as follows: the north section, which hasn't yet been fully excavated, is to the right; the central section is opposite; and the south section is to the left.

Pyramid of the Magician

The first and most prominent building you'll see is the almost oval-shaped pyramid, called the **Pyramid of the Magician** or **Dwarf**, its name derived from the legend that it was built in a single night by the son of a witch who had hatched him from an egg. The dwarf/magician had been ordered to construct a complete building by the next day or be put to death – a colorful story, reminiscent of Rumpelstiltskin and Merlin, that firmly fixes the name of the pyramid in one's mind. In reality, the building consists of five superimposed pyramids built over a period of centuries.

The most recent section is the tallest temple on top, the oldest at ground level at the back, with the intermediate structures in between. You can climb up very steep narrow steps to the top of the pyramid, holding on to a chain at the side, but getting back down is trickier than the climb up. You'll note all degrees of daring among people making the ascent and descent – some clinging fearfully to the chain, others zigzagging up or down at a fairly brisk pace, the way the Indians are said to have navigated the stairs. Although the view from the top is well worth the climb, don't despair if you aren't up to tackling the ascent, as there are other points at Uxmal where you can get a sweeping view of the ruins.

The unusually soft contours of this rounded pyramid were, according to one story, created so that Ehecatl, the god of the wind, wouldn't hurt himself on any sharp edges when he blew over the structure. Although 'archeologically incorrect' (Ehecatl was a god from the central highlands), the explanation is quite delightful – just the sort of thing an imaginative guide would invent and visitors would never forget.

Around the back of the pyramid we find a plaza formed by four buildings, the famous and photogenic **Nunnery Quadrangle**. This name dates from the 1600s when Friar Diego López de Cogolludo, having no other reference for its function and being reminded of the cloister of a Spanish convent, assigned it this name, which has stuck ever since. The use of these buildings isn't known but its 74 chambers suggest some sort of residence or school.

The Nunnery Quadrangle

The exquisite beauty of these Mayan buildings inspired the famous modern Mexican architect, Pedro Ramírez Vázquez, in the design of his magnificent Museum of Anthropology in Mexico City – in particular the pinkish stone, general proportions, and four separate buildings defining the interior quadrangle. The entire complex, built on an elevated, man-made platform, typifies the characteristics of the Puuc architectural style, based on the simple Mayan hut, the *na*, with its smooth walls and high-peaked thatched roof. (Here, you'll even see small huts sculpted on the facade of the west building, over the doorways.)

There's nothing simple, however, in the complexity of the stonework, which was created piece by piece following a master plan and interlocked like a three-dimensional jigsaw puzzle. Among the many other details (latticework, snakes, and so on), which your guide can explain to you, note in particular the scores of Chaac masks, often artfully placed on corners where his curved nose can be seen to best advantage silhouetted against the sky and seeming to pierce the clouds to bring life-giving rain. It's no accident that the rain god has been given such a prominent place, since this part of the Yucatán Peninsula not only has no rivers but even the *cenotes* or sinkholes are absent (although commonplace just a few miles

View of Uxmal

farther north). In Uxmal, water was collected from the rains and stored in *chaltunes*, bottle-shaped cisterns carved out of stone and sealed with thick coats of plaster.

Now head through the triangular arch of the south building to visit the structure considered even more beautiful than the Nunnery Quadrangle, the **Governor's Palace**. On the way north, you'll cross the remains of an unrestored ball court with a stone ring still embedded in one wall. Also note a building on the right with a series of perforated triangular roof crests that has been misnamed the **Dovecote** and was probably designed for astronomical sightings.

Ascend the very high platform that sets the palace off to perfection and also provides a panoramic viewpoint for visitors. Considered one of the masterpieces of all Mayan architecture, with its many doors, corbelled arches and gentle recesses, delicate proportions and the light and shadow created by its sculptured decoration, the palace certainly befits a ruler.

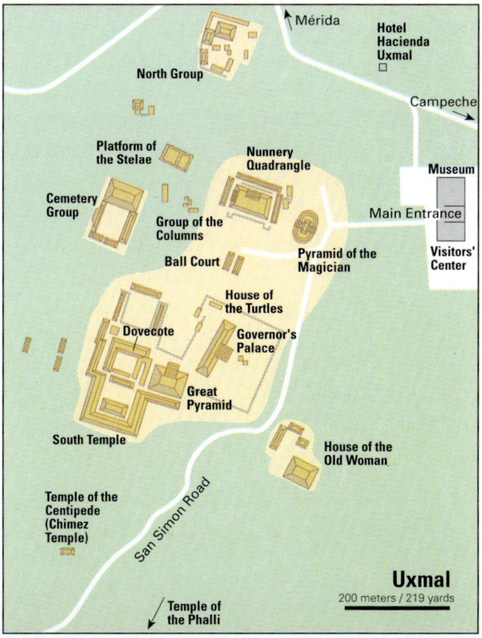

The majesty of this structure wasn't always visible. John Stephens tells of his second trip to Uxmal: 'Amid this mass of desolation, grand and stately as when we left it, stood the Casa del Gobernador, but with all its terraces covered, and separated from us by a mass of impenetrable verdure... The grass and weeds were above our heads and we could see nothing.' Frederick Catherwood's drawings,

Palace of the Masks at Kabáh

which were created after the impenetrable vegetation had eventually been cleared away, clearly show the arches filled with rubble.

Looking away from the palace, past the **two-headed jaguar throne**, imagine how everything must have looked when the road connecting this palace to Kabáh *(see below)* shone brightly in the sun.

Some other points to visit at Uxmal are: the **Great Pyramid**, behind the Governor's Palace, which hasn't been fully restored but is considered to be as tall as the Pyramid of the Magician and provides an even better view of the ruins; the **Temple of the Phalli**, to the right and and just ahead of the Governor's Palace, and the **House of the Old Woman** (the dwarf/magician's mother) in the direction of Kabáh. Little restoration work has been lavished on all these structures, so if your energy and time are limited, you can forgo them without missing much.

After covering everything you want to see, consider lunch at the Visitors' Center. Posher options are the Hotel Hacienda Uxmal on the other side of the highway (which has a big *comida corrida* for less than US $15 or a cheaper lunch under $10) or Las Palapas, around 3½km (2 miles) away on the road back to Mérida. It would be worthwhile staying overnight *(see Practical Information)* if you'd like to see the *son et lumière* (sound and light show). Check at the Visitors' Center for the time – there are two shows, one in Spanish, the other in English.

Note that many tours include nearby **Kabáh**, **Sayil** (noted for its palace) and **Labná** (its arch has two *na* houses incorporated into its reliefs) in a single package, in addition to Uxmal. Whether or not you decide to follow suit will depend on your threshold for ruins exhaustion.

If you do go on to visit Kabáh (about a mile from Uxmal), cross the road, away from the main temples, to reach a free-standing arch, where the road to Uxmal began.

Campeche

Escape from the throngs of tourists at many other sites on the Yucatán Peninsula by visiting leisurely Campeche, which still retains parts of the fortress walls which shielded it against pirate attacks in colonial times. Edzná and Jainá are the main archeological sites nearby.

9. Exploring Campeche

A half-day tour of Campeche. *See map on page 56.*

If you'd like to savor a small city off the main tourist track or are passing through on your way to other points of the Mayan world, visit Campeche (about 190km/150 miles southwest of Mérida on Highway 180). Located right on the sea, it has colorful colonial buildings and ramparts, as well as a new section on the seafront that's ultra-modern.

The rather provincial atmosphere of Campeche belies its former role as the peninsula's gateway of shipping, where galleons laden with gold and silver, as well as precious woods, set sail for Spain. Pirates were naturally attracted by these riches and established their headquarters at what is now Ciudad del Carmen, from where they launched raiding parties, not so much on the vessels as on the town. Such famous figures as John Hawkins, Henry Morgan and Francis Drake, to mention only the British pirates, repeatedly attacked the town.

The worst raid of all took place in 1663 when the buccaneers of several nations joined together in a ferocious onslaught, raping the women, slaughtering the populace and destroying buildings in an attack of unprecedented savagery. This finally led the Spanish crown to decide on the construction of 2.5-m (8-ft) thick walls, which eventually ringed the city, making it one of the few fortress cities in the Americas, a hexagonal

Campeche's Land Gate

stronghold guarded by eight towers. Faced with the now impregnable port, where shipping had to enter between the daunting walls, the pirates redirected their energies to easier prey. In 1717 an attack was led by Alonso Felipe de Aranda against the pirates on Isla del Carmen, which finally wiped them out, killing many and routing the rest.

Settled since the days of Maya hegemony, before the arrival of the Spanish, the village commanded both sea and overland trade routes between Yucatán and other civilizations in the rest of Mexico. The original name of *Ah Kim Pech* was transliterated by the Spanish to Campeche, when they founded the first European settlement on the site in 1517. Due to fierce Mayan resistance the Spanish didn't secure Campeche for themselves until 1542, under the leadership of Francisco de Montejo the Younger, who founded the city of Mérida the same year.

In the decades after Mexico's independence in 1821, when shipping to Spain was reduced to a trickle, Campeche became a backwater with an economy based on fishing. Its walls saved it again during the War of the Castes in the middle of the century, when Mayan insurgents had taken every town and city in the peninsula except Campeche and Mérida.

At the end of the century the *Campechanos*, deciding they no longer needed bulwarks against attacks and wanting to install trolley lines to areas outside the fortifications, began to dismantle them. However, the Puerta de Mar (Sea Gate), razed in the 19th century, was rebuilt in the 1950s when its value as a tourist attraction was realized. The oil boom of the 1970s brought new life to the city.

Today, colorful colonial buildings line the flagstoned streets of the compact downtown area, formerly within the fortress walls. Bulwark towers dot the townscape at regular intervals and the colors yellow and white are used generously throughout the city, an almost painterly touch symbolically reminiscent of the Indian yellow, for the sacred corn, and white for *atole*, a corn-based drink. The first-time visitor is struck by the number of statues, some seeming to gaze out to sea, the origin of so many of Campeche's historic events.

Campeche kids

The Catedral de la Concepción

Start in the old colonial plaza or **Parque Principal**, bordered by Calles 8 and 10, running roughly parallel to the coastline, and Calles 55 and 57, which intersect them perpendicularly. As in other Mexican towns, this plaza is the center of city life, where people congregate to enjoy the trees, band concerts and, of course, attend Mass in the **Catedral de la Concepción**, whose plain facade and tall twin towers are typical of the earliest churches on the peninsula. Its dome has curious flying buttresses radiating around it.

The large round **gazebo** in the center of the square is a modern creation. Note the old **Los Portales** building, with its graceful facade and arcade. One of the most dramatic buildings in the city is the former **Mansión Carvajal**, a luxurious design with undulating Moorish arches, striking black and white checked floors and sweeping staircase – attesting to the wealth that once flowed through the city. Entrance to the mansion is behind the cathedral on Calle 10 near Calle 53. Stores and offices are now located in this boldly designed house, as well as the *Museo de la Canción y del Compositor Campechano* (Museum of Campechan Song and Composers).

Posada in Campeche

Seven bulwarks *(baluartes)* of Campeche's old wall have been retained and are now used as public buildings for a variety of purposes. Take Calle 53 to the left of the Carvajal mansion, toward the sea, to reach the **Baluarte de Santiago**, now the site of the **Jardín Botánico**. Back outside, along the seafront, walk along the stretch of remaining wall to enter the **Baluarte Soledad** to see the Mayan stelai exhibited there. These slabs of stone brought from different sites were turned into vertical sculptures, often covered with hieroglyphs that have been of key importance in deciphering the ancient written

Fuerte de San Miguel

language. The accompanying drawings clarify the sometimes worn stone faces. The tall stone arched gate that you see is the rebuilt **Puerta de Mar** (Sea Gate).

Among the new buildings ahead is the **Congreso del Estado** – Campeche is a state capital – whose curious shape, reminiscent of a shelled oyster, has earned it the local nicknames of the UFO, the flying saucer and the sandwich. Next door is the **Baluarte de San Carlos**, housing the city museum, worth a visit to see the maps, photos and an architectural model of the town as it was with its walls intact. The bird's-eye view you'll get of the fortress town should orient you on the rest of your exploration.

Now, head inland on Circuito Baluartes Street, past the small statue to motherhood, to peek into the patio of the **Instituto Campechano** on Calle 65, a shiny-clean school with a proud staff. Returning to Baluartes, keep on until the **Baluarte de Santa Rosa**, soon to reopen as a historical museum.

To round out your coverage of this charming colonial city, keep on Circuito Baluartes to reach the **Baluarte de San Juan**, still connected to a stretch of fortification containing the **Puerta de Tierra** (Land Gate), the former entrance of the city for travelers coming overland. You can walk along the top of the wall and also check out the portraits of both city fathers and pirates, some of which are quite amusing to modern eyes. One of the largest and most attractive of Campeche's museums is nearby – the **Museo Regional de Campeche**, which has an extensive collection of Mayan items, scale models, clay figures and even the wooden contraption used to deform babies' heads to achieve the sharply sloping forehead that the Mayans considered a mark of beauty. You'll come away with insights into this fascinating culture. Located at Calle 59 No 36, the building was formerly the governor's house.

Campeche is famous both for its hospitality and its seafood. For lunch you might like the colonial atmosphere of **Restaurant Miramar** at Calle 8, No 203, near Calle 61 close to the Puerta de Mar

One of Campeche's many statues

(tel: 6-28-83); the popular and economical **Marganzo**, Calle 8, No 267 (tel: 1-38-98) serving excellent regional dishes; or **La Pigua**, Av Miguel Alemán 197-A (tel: 1-33-65) for a leisurely seafood lunch in a glass-walled dining room surrounded by trees and plants. The specialty is a local fish called *pejelagarto.*

After lunch take a drive along the waterfront en route to **Fuerte de San Miguel** (San Miguel's fort) from which there's a great view of the city. You might find time for some shopping – Campeche has excellent Panama hats, cattle-horn jewelry (that looks like tortoise shell) and nautical objects such as ships in bottles. Check the *Shopping* section for details. The local tourist office is most helpful and they have bilingual guides.

City tours are available, if you prefer a guided visit. They are located at Av Ruiz Cortines, across the street from the Palacio de Gobierno (tel: 6-55-93). Alternatively, check at your hotel or contact Viajes Potoncham, Calle 67, No 1, Apt 3B (tel: 6-67-96) or Viasetur, Calle 8, No 201 (tel: 1-40-20), noting that both close at lunchtime (around 2–3 or 4pm). Taking a hint from the locals, who close up shop for an extended lunch hour, try to schedule your explorations prior to the hours when the sun is directly overhead.

10. Edzná and Jainá

A choice of two Mayan sites easily accessible from Campeche. *See map on pages 18/19.*

Edzná was already an important city by 100AD, owing to its location on the main Mayan trading routes. It gradually developed an enormous hydraulic system that included over 16km (10 miles) of canals probably used for irrigation. The city continued to evolve over a thousand years and most of the buildings now standing date from the late Classic period, prior to the mysterious abandonment of Mayan cities around 900AD. The site is located some 50km (30 miles) southeast of Campeche (the highway through Chencoyí).

If you're not a real ruins buff, the site may not be very inspiring to visit, as only a small proportion has been excavated. The most notable structure is the **Main Temple**, standing in what has been described as the main acropolis, unique in that it was apparently used for dwellings – what look like windows are, in fact, the doors to the rooms. There are passageways on the first two stories under the stairs, a very unusual development. More than a score of groupings of buildings have been identified, so far.

Edzná Acropolis

View of Edzná from the Acropolis

Jainá, a small island north of Campeche, was the burial site of high-ranking people from all over the Mayan world, from the Classic period onward. It is most famous for the clay figurines that were buried with the dead. Only discovered in the 20th century by the great Mayanist Sylvanus Morley, the small-scale sculptures have been invaluable for their realistic portrayal of costumes and of how people lived. Before deciding on a visit, drop by the Museo Regional de Campeche to see some of these figures, as you won't see them at the site. Check with the travel agency in your hotel or one of those mentioned above about current conditions for visiting the island, as a permit is required from the Institute of Anthropology and History (INAH).

11. Campeche to Chetumal

This long journey to Chetumal, the capital of Quintana Roo, is a good option for anyone traveling on to Belize.
See map on pages 18/19.

For those who love exploration by car and are willing to drive well off the beaten tourist track, through long stretches of rather monotonous landscape, consider the trek from Campeche across the Yucatán Peninsula to Chetumal, the capital of Quintana Roo. Take Highway 261 south, aiming for Francisco Escárcega, where you'll connect to the east–west Highway 186, arriving in around three hours, a drive, like most in Mexico, best made in daylight. The 80-km (50-mile) stretch of curving coastline between Campeche and Champotón is notable for its popular swimming beaches, such as Seyba Playa and Siho

To Chetumal

Playa. Some off-shore rigs, oil being responsible for the region's current prosperity, as well as boats of the shrimp fleet for which it is still notable, can be seen off the coast. At the town of Champotón (population: 19,000) the road heads due south overland to Francisco Escárcega, where you'll connect with highway 186 for the 300-km (185-mile) drive east to Chetumal. Be sure to fill up your gas tank at every opportunity, as Pemex stations are scarce in this region and towns even more so.

The road extends over flat terrain flanked by a seemingly endless stretch of impenetrable, low-lying scrub forest – an uninviting scene for exploration, which may explain why major Mayan cities are still being discovered in the midst of this region. Among the archeological sites along the way are **Becán** and **Xpuhil**, both relatively close to the highway. Becán has a ball court of the type found at many other ancient centers. The ball game, mentioned in the *Popul Vuh*, one of the few surviving Mayan sacred books, was played with a hard rubber ball that had to be manipulated using only knees, hips and elbows to propel it through a small stone ring attached to the wall. Although to our eyes the game seems like an early version of a modern team sport, it actually had a deep religious significance, perhaps related to fertility rites and involving various ceremonies and rituals.

Kohunlich's Pyramid of the Masks

Calakmul, in the midst of a biosphere reserve, claims the tallest pyramid of the entire Mayan world. **Río Bec** is the name of both a site and an architectural style, characterized by pyramids so steep that the sides are marked with horizontal strips as decoration instead of stairs, since the structures could not be ascended. **Kohunlich** is the relatively unexcavated site in the vicinity of Chetumal, famous for its **Pyramid of the Masks** and a large area which the early inhabitants used to collect rainwater.

The main attraction of all these tranquil places, surrounded by jungle, is their lack of tourists – they are inaccessible without a car and the road to Río Bec is sometimes almost impassable. There

Chetumal's corniche

is still much to be excavated and merely to visit any of these ruins is an adventure, although with promotion of the Maya Route they may some day be as populous as Uxmal and Chichén-Itzá.

The Mayan era reached its highest point of development between 300 and 900AD, before declining for reasons that are still unclear. Then came a hiatus of nearly a millennium during which most of the once glorious cities were swallowed up by the jungle. Serious excavations did not begin until the 19th century.

Though the state capital of Quintana Roo, **Chetumal** itself (population: 92,000) does not have very much to detain visitors. But it is beautifully situated on a vast bay and goods have been shipped from its harbor since ancient times, when the Mayans conducted a thriving export trade in cacao and imported precious metals. Today's exports are mostly mahogany and other hardwoods from nearby forests. The modern appearance of this ancient port with its wide boulevards and duty-free shops is due to its reconstruction after disastrous hurricanes in 1942 and 1955.

There are inexpensive hotels near the bus station, about 10 blocks north of the waterfront, but the best place is the Hotel Holiday Inn Puerta Maya on Av Héroes, with its pool and air-conditioning.

Before leaving Chetumal, it's worth the one-hour bus ride to inspect the 18th-century fortress at **Bacalar**, a tiny town on the far side of the *laguna* (lagoon) of the same name, which felt the need to build adequate defenses after being sacked by pirates in the 17th century. Bacalar was the first colonial settlement in what is now the state of Quintana Roo. Its turquoise waters are popular for both fishing and boat trips.

Family outing

To reach the **Sian Ka'an Biosphere Reserve** to the north, take Highway 307. Don't miss the villages of **Punta Allen** and **Boca Paila**, which are incorporated into the reserve and offer basic accommodation. (Call the Amigos de Sian Ka'an in Cancún on 84-95-83 for further information.)

Bacalar Laguna

Shopping

Almost no one comes away from Mexico without having purchased at least one example of the country's enormous variety of arts and crafts. Many return home laden down with treasures. Visitors to Yucatán can choose from the typical products of the area as well as items from other regions of Mexico. Do a little comparison shopping first, to get an idea of the range of goods, quality and prices, unless you see something you fall in love with and absolutely must have.

Panama hats

Campeche

While definitely not a shopping destination, check out the **Baluarte San Pedro**, Circuito Baluartes and Calle 16, for general arts and crafts. Look especially for the famous *jipi* hats, excellent quality handwoven Panamas. Afterwards, check out the local **market**, which is right across the street, for all sorts of groceries, including local tropical fruits and vegetables, plus household goods. Now walk back towards the Zócalo on Calle 53, and just past the cathedral turn left on Calle 8 to reach **Artesanía Típica Naval**, between Calles 59 and 67, in front of Baluarte La Soledad, for their own designs of miniature ships, jewelry and decorative objects made of coral, shell and horn (which looks like tortoiseshell) and other pieces of a nautical inspiration. **La Casa de las Artesanías Tukulna**, Calle 10, operated by the government-run Family Institute (DIF), has an excellent selection of regional crafts.

Cancún

In one or another of the many malls in the hotel zone, you should find just about anything you want, from imported brand names, pricey Mexican arts and crafts targeted at the discriminating shopper with a large budget, to the usual variety of inexpensive items. For a mall-hopping tour, start in the heart of the hotel zone at Punta Cancún on Blvd Kukulcán Km 8.5 by the Centro de Convenciones, for a visit to **Plaza Caracol**, whose 200 shops and restaurants will provide an excellent introduction to what's available (such as Ronay,

The accent is on abstracts

for exclusive jewelry). Cross the street for a visit to the Plaza La Fiesta, Blvd Kukulcán Km 9, to take a closer look at the brilliantly colored Guatemalan textiles, many of them in needlepoint, plus a wide variety of arts and crafts from all over Mexico.

For evening shopping mixed with entertainment head for the **Party Center**'s stores, restaurants, nightclubs and bars next to the Convention Center on the other side of Kukulcán. Don't miss the unique creations at **Galería de Sergio Bustamante** in the Fiesta Americana Coral Beach, for surrealistic sculptures and jewelry by one of Mexico's most famous artists. Head to Km 11 on the lagoon side of the street for the **Flamingo Plaza**, distinguished by Mayan arches in its modern facade, for a full range of stores (peek into **La Casa del Habaño** for Cuban cigars), restaurants, *casas de cambio* (for changing foreign currency) and travel agencies.

Continue on to Km 13 to wind up at the large **Kukulcán Plaza** (pick up that special item to wear in the evening at **Mezza Luna**, where you will find spectacular locally made bustiers with hand-painted appliqués).

Cozumel

One of Cozumel's main offerings to shoppers is jewelry, often in silver or coral – you should examine everything to determine that it's genuine and not a high-priced fake, especially items on the street. Stroll around Av Rafael Melgar and the main plaza to get an overview of what's available. Check out the **Mercado de Artesanías**, at the corner of Calle 1 Sur and Av 5 Sur, where you'll see many arts and crafts outlets under one roof, market-style, and can compare prices. Dive shops are ubiquitous south of town.

Isla Mujeres

Walk around the Zócalo and nearby streets to get an idea of the number and range of gift shops on the island, besides checking out what the street vendors are hawking. One of the most eclectic shops for quality folk art is **Casablanca**, Av Rafael Melgar, 33. For fine jewelry, head over to Av Rafael Melgar 101 to **Rachat and Romero**.

Mérida

Mérida has lower prices than Cancún for pretty much everything. Well-made hammocks, the best in the country; men's *guayabera* shirts, the tropical substitute for a jacket and tie (they're worn outside the pants), are white cotton and decorated with tucks; women's colorful *huipiles*, the loose-fitting, brightly embroidered white tunic blouses worn over a matching skirt, ranging from costly (several hundred dollars) pure cotton, totally hand-worked examples to inexpensive but attractive polyester, machine-embroidered models. Go to the **Mercado de Artesanías** (part of the main market but in its own building), Calle 67 at Calle 56, and check out the main market itself for local color. Then head to Calle 58 No 604, at Calle 73, to check out the selection of hammocks at **El Aguacate**. Reputed to be the best in the world, Yucatecan hammocks are very stable – you actually wrap yourself in them. Look for pure cotton or linen thread, as synthetics can be scratchy, and check carefully to see that the weaving is even. They are sold in sizes named after regular beds, and some can sleep several people. Ask for assistance in measuring a hammock to your height and weight and inquire about the necessary hardware for safe hanging. Calle 60 is a good street for stores – continue right down to the Zócalo, browsing along the way. For fine arts and crafts, visit the **La Casa de Artesanías**, Calle 63 No 503, between Calles 64 and 66, picturesquely housed in a restored monastery, five blocks from the Zócalo.

Eye-catching rugs

Archeological Sites

Check out the stores at the main sites, such as Chichén-Itzá and Uxmal, where you will find books in several languages; a limited number of reproduction items; a variety of arts and crafts; and clothing, some quite unusual. You may be pleasantly surprised by some of the upscale shops, such as **Georgia** at Uxmal, where you can find imaginative women's skirts, blouses and accessories designed by an artist.

Eating Out

Mexico offers a gastronomical adventure into what is considered one of the world's three major cuisines, the others being French and Chinese. A combination of pre-Hispanic cooking methods and ingredients (chilies, tomatoes, beans, all forms of tortillas, avocados, chocolate, peanuts and more) and European contributions (including rice, wheat, beef, pork, onion, citrus fruits and bananas), ensure each meal is an adventure. You don't need to spend a lot of money to sample tasty, nutritious food. Each region has its own dishes and since you're in the Yucatán Peninsula, you should try some of the local specialties: for example *sopa de limón* (chicken soup, with tortilla and a squeeze of lime juice); *cochinita pibil* (cured pork baked in banana leaves), served as tacos in tortillas with onions marinated in orange juice and optional chili, otherwise known as *pollo pibil* when it is made with chicken; *papadzules* (chopped hard-boiled eggs wrapped in a tortilla and covered in a delicious pumpkin seed sauce). You will also find some exotic foreign cuisines. Some of the best restaurants in Mérida, for example, offer both Yucatecan and Lebanese dishes, thanks to the many Lebanese immigrants.

This list that follows is only a brief sampling of many Yucatecan delights. See what's on the menu and go for an adventurous choice. Prices per person, without drinks: $ = under US$15; $$ = US$15–25; $$$ = over US$25.

Dining on the 'playa'

Campeche

La Pigua
Av Miguel Alemún 197-A
Tel: 1-33-65
Excellent seafood served in a glass-walled dining room surrounded by trees and plants. $$

Las Cucharas
Calle 16, 148
Tel: 1-02-24
Varied local cuisine with some surprising mixtures of tastes. $

Stained-glass decor

Restaurant Bar Marganzo
Calle 8, 267
Tel: 1-38-98
Good Mexican food, which is served by hostesses dressed in regional costumes. This is a perennial upscale favorite. $$

Restaurant La Parroquia
Calle 55, 9
Tel: 6-80-86
La Parroquia is open 24 hours a day, and offers an extensive menu. Soak up the local atmosphere in this much-loved café. $

Restaurant Miramar,
Calle 8, 203, near Calle 61
Tel: 6-28-83
Good place to sample Campeche's famous seafood as well as numerous Mexican dishes. $$

Cancún

Each hotel on Cancún island offers several dining options and there are scores of independent restaurants of all nationalities. In fact, no vacation is long enough to try out the hundreds of possibilities.

Cancún Hotel Zone

Casa Rolandi
Plaza Caracol Shopping Center, Km 8
Tel: 83-18-17
Italian and Swiss dishes served in a lively atmosphere. $$

La Joya
Fiesta Americana Coral Beach Hotel
Tel: 83-29-00
Excellent Mexican and international dishes. One of Cancún's finest (and most expensive) restaurants. $$$

100% Natural
Plaza Terramar
Tel: 83-11-80
Delicious health food 24 hours a day in pleasant atmosphere. $$

Señor Frog's
Blvd Kukulcán, Km 8.5, Plaza Lagunas
Tel: 3-29-31
Offers a festive atmosphere and good food. $$

Señor Frog's

ZUPPA
Plaza Kukulcán
Tel: 83-29-66
Superb Italian cooking. Desserts are a real treat. $$$

Downtown Cancún

LA HABICHUELA
Margaritas 25
Tel: 84-31-58
Old favorite serving international and regional fare in a romantic setting. Also offers dinner cruises. $$–$$$

LOS ALMENDROS
Av Bonampak Sur (corner Sayil, front of bullring)
Tel: 83-30-93
Color photo menu of house Yucatecan dishes such as lime soup and *cochinita pibil*. $$

PERICO'S
Av Yaxchilán, 71
(between Cobá and Sunyaxchen)
Tel: 84-31-52
Lively, fun atmosphere for tasty Mexican, seafood and steaks. $$

TACOLOTE
Blvd Kukulcán Km 3.5
Tel: 87-30-45
Try famous *tacos al carbón* (charcoal grilled beef, chopped for easy eating in soft, warm tortillas) among other varieties. $$

YAMAMOTO
Plaza Kukulcán
Tel: 87-33-66
Traditional Japanese cuisine in the unlikely setting of Mexico. $$$

Chichén-Itzá

HOTEL HACIENDA CHICHÉN-ITZA
Close to southern entrance to site
Tel: 1-00-45
The house where the first archeological teams lived. Beautiful setting. $$

HOTEL MAYALAND
Situated just outside the southern entrance to the ruins, next to Hotel Hacienda Chichén
Tel: 1-00-77
This hotel has a choice of three restaurants. It has a dignified, formal ambiance. $$

PIRAMIDE INN
Tel: 1-01-15
Good restaurant located in a motel. $

Cobá

EL BOCADITO
Main street in village
Casual, spartan restaurant popular with tour groups. $

VILLA ARQUEOLOGICA
Near entrance to ruins on Lake Cobá
Tel: 4-20-87
Refined Gallic atmosphere and cuisine, plus Yucatecan dishes. $$

Cozumel

EL ARRECIFE
Presidente Inter-Continental Hotel.
Tel: 2-03-22
Excellent Italian and Mediterranean specialties with an ocean view. $$$

LA CHOZA (THE GRILL)
Calle Rosado Salas 198 at Av 10 Norte
Tel: 2-09-58
Great Mexican food. Has been awarded the best restaurant rating by *Food and Wine Magazine* in the past. $$

PEPE'S GRILL
Av Rafael Melgar, 220
Tel: 2-02-13 (reservation suggested)

Ocean views from María's Kan Kin

Mellow atmosphere and great food. Ideal for a splurge when you're feeling extravagant. $$$

Isla Mujeres

MARIA'S KAN KIN
Km 4 Carretera al Garrafón
Tel: 7-00-15

On the beach

French cuisine under a *palapa* overlooking the sea. Live lobsters. $$

MIRTITA'S
Av Rueda Medina (near dock)
Good but unpretentious eatery. $

PIZZA ROLANDI
Hidalgo between Abasolo and Madero
Tel: 7-04-30
Delicious Italian dishes and good pizza. $$

ZAZIL-HA
Na-Balam Hotel
Tel: 7-02-79
Fine cuisine includes regional specialties, seafood and vegetarian dishes in lovely beachside setting. Gracious service. $$

Mérida

ALBERTO'S CONTINENTAL PATIO
Calle 64 and Calle 57
Tel: 28-63-36
Alberto's offers both international and Lebanese dishes. Particularly recommended for that expensive and elegant evening you've been saving your pesos for. $$–$$$

CAFETERIA POP
Calle 57 No 501 between Calles 60 and 62
Tel: 28-61-63
A longtime favorite, particularly with students. Really good breakfasts. $

EL MESON
Parque Hidalgo (Calle 60)
Tel: 24-90-22
This is the place to go for a long al fresco lunch. In the corner of a charming plaza. $–$$

La Bella Época
Calle 60, 497 Hotel del Parque (between Calles 57 and 59)
Tel: 24-78-44
You can choose between international, Mayan or vegetarian dishes. Pleasant ambiance made even more agreeable by the sound of a piano. $$

Santa Lucia
Calle 60 No 481 (next to Santa Lucía park)
Tel: 28-81-35
Full course meals featuring Yucatecan favorites. $

Los Almendros
Calle 50, 493 (between Calles 57 and 59)
Tel: 23-81-35
The traditional choice for Yucatecan specialties. $$

Tulúm

Casa Cenote
On dirt road off Highway 307, between Xel-Há and Tulúm.
A fine restaurant beside a *cenote*. Delicious fajitas and seafood kebabs. $$

Cabañas Ana y José
On a dirt road off Highway 307 between entrance to the ruins and town.
One of the best in the area. $$

Uxmal

Hotel Hacienda Uxmal
Carretera 261, Km 80
Tel: 99/24-71-42
A choice of restaurants in this beautiful four-star hotel, located just across from the ruins. $$

Restaurant-Bar Yax Beh
Visitors' Center at ruins
Eat among other tired but elated travelers enjoying the air-conditioning. Right on the site, with rather expensive prices. $$

Villa Arqueologica
Entry road just by ruins' parking lot
Tel: 99/29-70-53
Club Med for French food. Cultural setting. $$

Valladolid

El Bazar
Calles 40 and 39, at corner of Zócalo
A series of simple eateries, all offering a variety of tasty, economical food. $

El Meson del Marqués
Calle 39, 203
Tel: 6-20-73
On main plaza next to Hotel del Marqués. Offers Mexican and Yucatecan dishes. $$

Simple dining in Campeche

Nightlife

The two main centers for lively entertainment on the peninsula are Cancún (glitzy) and Mérida (rather more cultural), although Cozumel is also good for discos.

Campeche

This is a true provincial city and entertainment options for late nights are few, but dancing is one possibility.

Discos

Try **Disco Atlantis**, Hotel Ramada, Av Ruíz Cortínes, 51; **La Calle 8**, Calle 8, Downtown, is open Fridays and Saturdays.

Check at your hotel or the tourist office for dates and times of folk music and dance performances at different plazas in the city.

Cancún

Cancún's nightlife is generally expensive (in particular, be prepared for stiff cover charges) but the sheer variety of options will keep you busy every night, if you manage to keep up the pace.

Bars / Restaurants

Carlos 'n' Charlie's, lagoon side of Blvd Kukulcán, near Calinda Beach hotel; the ever-popular **Señor Frog's**, lagoon side of Blvd Kukulcán, near Casa Maya hotel; **Carlos O'Brian's**, Av Tulúm, downtown Cancún, all have dance floors.

If you would like to combine eating out with a romantic cruise, there are several companies offering floating dinner cruises. Pleasant options include **Columbus**, on a galleon-style boat (tel: 83-14-88); **Lobster Sunset Cruise** (tel: 83-04-00); **Pirate's Night Adventure** (tel: 83-14-88).

Folk Dance

Ballet Folklórico Nacional de México, Hotel Continental Villas Plaza, Blvd Kukulcán (tel: 83-10-22). This is an unforgettable performance of Mexican folk dances executed by some of the region's best professionals. The evening's entertainment also includes supper, and you will need to make reservations as far in advance as possible. There's a dinner show featuring a fine performance by the Flying Indians of Papantla dancers at Xcaret (tel: 83-07-65).

Tricks of the trade

Dancing till dawn

Discos

Coco Bongo, Blvd Kukuicán, Km 9.5, **Fat Tuesday**, Blvd Kukulcán 6.5 (tel: 83-26-76); **Christine**, Hotel Krystal, Blvd Kukulcán, Km 7.5 (tel: 83-11-33); **Daddy'O**, Blvd Kukulcán, Km 9.5 (tel: 83-31-34) and **Daddy Rock**, next door (tel: 83-16-26); **Hard Rock Café**, Blvd Kukulcán, Km 8.5 (tel: 83-20-24). **La Boom**, Blvd Kukulcán, Km 3.5 (tel: 83-14-58).

Music

Jazz: Casis Bar, Hotel Hyatt Cancún Caribe, Blvd Kukulcán, Km 10.5; **Pat O'Brien's**, Flamingo Plaza, Blvd Kukulcán, Km 11 (tel: 83-08-32). Cancún branch of the famous New Orleans bar. One bar is devoted to jazz; the other two offer rock and country.

Reggae: Try **Cat's**, Plaza Kukulcán, (tel: 83-19-10).

Romantic music for dancing: Find this at **The Touch of Class**, Centro de Convenciones, Blvd Kukulcán, Km 9 (tel: 83-28-80).

Salsa and other Latin rhythms: Best at **Azucar**, next to the Hotel Camino Real at Punta Cancún in the hotel zone (tel: 83-04-41); and **Mango Tango**, on the lagoon side of Blvd Kukulcán, near Cancún Palace Hotel (tel: 85-03-03).

The lobby bars of hotels are also good places to find all kinds of live music. **Hotel Camino Real Cancún**, Blvd Kukulcán, Punta Cancún, for Mexican music in the evening or try **Hotel Fiesta Americana Coral Beach**, Blvd Kukulcán, Km 9.5, for easy listening music; the **Hotel Meliá Cancún**, Blvd Kukulcán, Km 14, for Latin rhythms; **Hotel Marriott Casamagna**, Blvd Kukulcán, Km 20, for lively, great *mariachi* music or **Hotel Sierra Cancún**, Blvd Kukulcán, Km 10, for Mexican trio music.

Party Center

Party Center, Blvd Kukulcán, Km. 9. A whole mall dedicated to parties, with stores open until 10pm, and restaurants, bars and nightclubs serving until 4–5am.

Cozumel

Visitors to Cozumel are generally more oriented to watersports, especially diving, and nightlife is more low-key than in Cancún. Divers like to retire early and be relatively fresh for the next day's explorations.

Bars / Restaurants

Carlos 'n' Charlie's, Av Melgar, 11 (tel: 2-01-91); **The Sports Page**, Av 5 Norte and Calle 2 (tel: 2-11-99). The latter is a well-known video bar for American sports events and reasonable food.

Bar baroque in Mérida

Dance

Forum, Av Circunvalación. Nightly Mexican fiesta with dance performances and *mariachi* bands. Check at your hotel for dates, times and reservations.

Discos

Neptuno, Av Rafael Melgar (tel: 2-15-37); **Hard Rock**, Rafael Melgar 2-A (tel: 2-52-71) has a good atmosphere and very lively dance floor.

Isla Mujeres

Isla attracts people looking for a slower pace and so its evening entertainment options are limited. Beach parties are popular with some tourists.

You might try the bar at the **Na-Balam Hotel** or **El Pinguino**, at the Posada del Mar.

Mérida

Free events are offered most days of the week with special events planned on Sundays as part of "Domingo en Mérida" program. Events are well publicized, especially around the Zócalo. Check start times carefully.

Monday: Regional *vaquería* (cowboy) show, with typical dancing and dress, at the **Palacio Municipal** on the main plaza (Zócalo).

Tuesday: 1940s big band music at the **Musical Memories Concert**, featuring hits by Glenn Miller and Benny Goodman, in Santiago Park, in front of the Rex movie theater.

Wednesday: String instruments and piano concerts at the **Casa de Artesanías** on Calle 63, between Calles 64 and 66.

Thursday: La Serenata (serenade) in **Santa Lucía park** for a fine display of typical Yucatecan dress, dance, music and folklore, on Calle 60, corner of Calle 55.

Friday: University students' serenade at the **Universidad de Yucatán**, between Calle 60 and Calle 57.

Saturday: Catholic Mass is held in English at the Santa Lucía church in Santa Lucía park at 6pm at Calle 60 and Calle 55.

Sunday: From 9am–9pm the streets surrounding the Zócalo are closed to traffic. Concerts are held at nearby municipal buildings, and you will find street theater and sidewalk vendors selling food, balloons, handicrafts and good souvenirs. Don't miss the bazaar in Santa Lucía park.

Discos and Nightclubs

La Hach, Fiesta Americana Hotel, Paseo de Montejo and Av Colón (tel: 20-21-94) and **Pancho's**, Calle 59 located between Calles 60 and 62 (tel: 23-09-42).

Calendar of Special Events

Although most festivals are centered on a sacred celebration, they aren't totally solemn affairs but a combination of religious fervor and dancing, music, feasting, and fireworks. Participation of the local people is complete, with everyone wearing their best clothes or special costumes designed for the occasion.

Festivals often last for several days; if you want to stay overnight at a festival site, hotel reservations should be made in advance. Remember that many Mayas dislike people taking their photo, so be sure to ask permission first, and respect their wishes. Every day in Mérida offers a celebration of some sort: check the *Nightlife* section for a full listing of daily activities.

JANUARY – MARCH

1 January: **New Year's celebration**, throughout region.

6: **Santos Reyes**, Three Kings/ Epiphany. Children receive gifts of toys and candy. Still a strong tradition despite the influence of Santa Claus.

10: **Virgin of Buctzotz** (Buctzotz, Yucatán State).

21: **Fiesta** (Dzitás, Yucatán).

1–5 February: **San Felipe** (San Felipe, Yucatán).

2: **Candelaría Corn Fair** (Tzucacab, Yucatán).

Carnival, Mardi Gras, with varying levels of festivity, depending on the city. A movable feast, it sometimes occurs in February.

16–21 March: **Spring Fair** (José María Morelos, Quintana Roo).

21 **Spring equinox**: Light provides descending serpent effect at Kukulcán pyramid in Chichén-Itzá. Witnessed by thousands. (Also see *Fall equinox* in September.)

Holy Week: This is celebrated everywhere in Mexico.

Good Friday: Dramatization of events of Crucifixion and burial of Christ in Mérida and towns of Acanceh, Baca and others.

Festival ensemble

At the hammock fair, Tekom

APRIL – MAY

3 April: **San Ildefonso** (Izamal, Yucatán State).
5: **Tobacco fair** (Ticul).
13–17: **Honey Fair** (Hopechnén).
15: **Ascension of Christ Fair** (Progreso, Yucatán).
26: Beginning of **Festival of the Holy Cross** (Quintana Roo).
Last week of April: **Isla Mujeres annual boat regatta**.
1–3 May: **Festival of the Holy Cross** (Felipe Carrillo Puerto, Quintana Roo, Cozumel).
5: **Anniversary of founding of city** (Chetumal, Quintana Roo).
12–18: **Chankah Veracruz**, in honor of the Immaculate Conception of the Virgin Mary (near Felipe Carrillo Puerto, Quintana Roo).
20: **Hammock fair** in town of Tekom.

JUNE – AUGUST

June: **Navy Day** (Quintana Roo). Exact date varies annually.
22–4: **Saint John the Baptist** (Campeche).
24–9: **Saints Peter and Paul** (Cozumel, Campeche).
25 July: **Saint James the Apostle** (Río Lagartos, Yucatán). Saint Christopher (Quintana Roo).
15 August: **Our Lady of Izamal** (Izamal, Yucatán).
20: **Traditional Fair** (Maní, Yucatán).

SEPTEMBER – OCTOBER

16 September: **Saint Ramón** (Izamal, Yucatán; Campeche).
21: **Fall equinox**: ascending serpent sunlight effect at Kukulcán pyramid in Chichén-Itzá.
24–9: **Celebration of San Miguel**, patron saint of the town of San Miguel (Cozumel).
27: **Cristo de las Ampollas**, Christ of the Blisters (Mérida).
4 October: **San Francisco de Asís** in villages near Mérida (Uman, Hocaba, Conkal and Telchac Puerto and Pueblo)
Annual October festival, Otoño Cultural, in Mérida (date varies). Theater, dance, art and some exchange of events with annual Cervantes festival in the city of Guanajuato.
18–28: **Cristo de Sitilpech** (Izamal). Major festival complete with fireworks, especially on 25th.
31: **All Souls' Eve**, celebrated all over the peninsula by taking offerings to graves of loved ones.

NOVEMBER – DECEMBER

1–2 November: **Day of the Dead** or **Hanal-Pixan** as it is known in the Yucatán. One of Mexico's most important traditions to honor the dead. The festivities include *ofrendas* (colorful altars to honor the deceaed) and gatherings in cemeteries where families take their loved ones' favorite foods to share with the dead. Interesting, and not morbid.
First 2 weeks in November: **X'matkuil Fair**, at former henequen *hacienda* 8km (5 miles) from Mérida. Horse competitions, bullfights, and more.
4–8 December: **Fair** in Campeche.
8: **Feast of the Immaculate Conception** of the Virgin Mary (Izamal, Celestun, Champotón).
12: **Feast of the Virgin of Guadalupe**. In honor of Mexico's patron saint.
16–24: **Posadas** (Inn) celebrations reenacting Mary and Joseph's quest for a place to stay.

Practical Information

GETTING THERE

By Air

International visitors traveling from the US, Canada and Cuba can fly directly into Cancún, while those proceeding from Europe, Asia, Australia, South America and other regions arrive at Mexico City, where they must take a connecting flight to Cancún or another chosen destination in the Yucatán Peninsula. There is also a shuttle service between such points as Cancún and Cozumel. All the airports are modern, with a taxi service available outside. To reconfirm your reservations, always a sensible precaution, call at least 24 hours before your flight. The airline phone numbers for the major Yucatán destinations are as follows:

Campeche: Aeroméxico (tel: 6-66-56).

Ciudad del Carmen: Mexicana and affiliates Aerocaribe, Aerocozumel and Aeroliteral (tel: 2-11-71).

Cancún: American (tel: 83-44-61); Continental (tel: 86-00-40); Cubana (tel: 86-01-92); Northwest (tel: 86-00-46); United (tel: 86-00-25); Aerocozumel (tel: 84-20-00); Aeroméxico (tel: 84-10-97); Mexicana (tel: 87-44-44); Aerocancún (tel: 86-02-25).

Cozumel: Mexicana (tel: 2-29-45). Shuttle from Cancún: Aerocozumel/Aerocaribe (tel: 2-08-77).

Mérida: Continental (tel: 46-13-90); Aeroméxico (tel: 27-90-00); Mexicana, along with its three affiliates Aerocaribe, Aerocozumel and Aeroliteral (tel: 24-66-33).

By Rail

It is no longer possible to travel by rail. Due to privatization there are only two or three passenger services in the whole of Mexico.

By Road

Mexico has an excellent highway system covering the nation. If you choose to drive from Mexico City, calculate 2–3 days on the road, depending on your speed and how many hours you drive per day, including overnight stays at points on the way. Once in Campeche, for example, distances are not so great – Mérida is 3 hours away; Chichén-Itzá is 1½ hours from Mérida; Cancún is 3 hours from Chichén-Itzá; Cozumel is 2½ hours from Cancún (including 1½ hours to find and take a ferry). Highways in the Yucatán are generally as straight as ancient Roman roads, due to the lack of hills. There are rest stops at every toll both on the fast highways, but few places to stop on the 'free' roads, so fill your tank when you can and take lots of water and snacks. If you fly in and want to rent a car, each city has a number of options available *(see the Getting Around section, page 79)*.

There are many bus lines serving the area but the first-class carriers are best, due to the heat (they're air-conditioned)

Local license

and the comfort (on-board movies and restroom, good maintenance). Reservations should be made in advance at the bus station. The ADO line provides service to most places and at the terminal you'll notice some other attractive lines, each with its own ticket counter and some with private waiting rooms. The addresses of bus stations in the main Yucatán destinations follow, plus two reliable carriers, although there are others that provide several daily departures for most destinations.

Campeche – Calle 45 and Gobernadores: ADO (tel: 6-34-65).

Cancún – Av Tulúm and Uxmal: ADO (tel: 84-13-78); Autotransportes del Caribe (tel: 07-41-74).

Mérida – Calle 69, 554: ADO (tel: 24-05-17); Omnibus Caribe Interpeninsular (tel: 45-07-44).

TRAVEL ESSENTIALS

When to Visit / Weather

The temperatures are balmy year-round, with an average of 26°C (80°F) but nights can get cool. The rainy season, from May to November, brings momentary relief but increases the humidity. The high tourist season is late December to April, with a smaller peak in the summer months. If you want less crowded conditions, come to Yucatán in the off season, when it's also a lot cheaper.

Visas

People from most countries will need a tourist card as well as valid passport, with visa to enter Mexico. Canadian and US citizens need only a tourist card or FMT (obtained at the airport) upon presenting proof of citizenship (birth certificate, passport, voter's registration or military ID), which is valid for 30, 60, 90 or 180 days. It's wise to ask for more time than you think you'll need to avoid the red tape involved in obtaining an extension.

Staying cool

Clothing

Bring summerwear, but be sure to carry a sweater against the chill of air-conditioned areas, including buses and restaurants, and cool nights. Save your most revealing clothes for the resorts, and wear conservative clothes in cities.

Electricity

110 volts, 60-cycle alternating current as in the US. There are sometimes outages or fluctuations.

Time Zone

The Yucatán Peninsula is on central standard time, 6 hours behind GMT. Daylight Saving Time is from May to September.

GETTING ACQUAINTED

Geography and Population

The northern region of the Yucatán Peninsula is flat, barely rising above sea level, covered with scrub jungle, with no rivers running above ground. Water is therefore scarce, but the land's porous limestone surface has led to the collapse of many underground caves, resulting in round sinkholes with water at the bottom. Surrounded on three sides by sea, the Gulf of Mexico on the west and north and the Caribbean on the east, the coastlines have been developed into prime holiday resort destinations.

Politically divided into three Mexican states: Yucatán, Campeche and Quintana Roo, the population comprises people of Spanish, Spanish-Indian *(mestizo)* and Mayan Indian descent.

MONEY MATTERS

The Mexican peso has been 'floating' since the 1994 devaluation and, although strongly denied by government officials, there are constant rumors of another. Exchange rates fluctuate continually, but are currently hovering at 9.50 Mexican pesos to one US dollar, 6.70 pesos to one Canadian dollar, and 14 pesos to the pound.

Mexican currency comes in denominations of 20, 50, 100 and 500 peso bills. Coins come in denominations of 1, 2, 5, 10 and 20 pesos and 5, 10, 20 and 50 centavos. The 20 peso coins have only recently been reintroduced, so be careful because the only valid coins are the 2000-2001 series. Getting change is always a headahce in Mexico, so use big bills in hotels and restaurants, saving coins for street vendors and transportation.

To simplify the conversion of prices into US dollars, request a conversion card, available for free in most hotels.

Foreign currency from a number of countries can be changed at the many exchange houses called *Casas de Cambio*. Rates vary from one to the other – if you're in an area where there are several (Av Tulúm in downtown Cancún, for example), check out the rates table posted inside to see which gives you the best deal. Money can also be changed at your hotel and in some places you can pay with dollars. In both cases, the rate will be less favorable to you. Major international credit cards are accepted. If lost or stolen they can be replaced (in the case of American Express usually within 24 hours).

GETTING AROUND

Taxis and Buses

Taxis are numerous in every location and cheap by US standards. Agree the price before departing in places that don't use a meter – most don't.

There is an extensive network of bus lines traveling between the cities, and city public transport systems are cheap and reliable. Inquire at your hotel on the routes to take you around town.

Car Rentals

There are several options for renting a car in each of the major cities in the peninsula. Prices range from US$30–70 per day, depending on the type of car, with insurance. If you plan to rent in one destination and return the car in another, check first to see what the extra charge is, as it can be quite hefty.

The following list gives the phone numbers for three US companies operating in the main cities, but there are many more local agencies you can check out to compare prices. Always check the condition of the cars available.

Cancún: Avis (tel: 86-01-47); Budget (tel: 84-02-04); Dollar (tel: 86-01-79); Hertz (tel: 87-66-44).
Cozumel: Avis (tel: 2-00-99); Dollar (tel: 2-44-46); Budget (tel: 2-17-42).
Mérida: Avis (tel: 84-21-35); Budget (tel: 46-22-55); Hertz (tel: 24-28-34).

HOURS AND HOLIDAYS

Business Hours

Banking hours are usually 9am–5pm in the cities, and until 1pm in smaller towns. Some offices and stores close for a long lunch hour from 2–4pm, and then stay open until 8pm. Larger stores and shopping malls stay open throughout the day until 8 or 9pm (even later in Cancún).

Public Holidays

Banks, government offices, schools, and stores are generally closed on the following dates; be sure to call in advance to find out if specific places are open:

Clearly signed

January 1	**New Year's Day**
February 5	**Constitution Day**
March 21	**Birthday of Benito Juárez**
Date Varies	**Easter**
May 1	**Labor Day**
September 1	**Informe Presidencial** *(President's Annual Report)*
September 16	**Independence Day**
October 12	**Día de la Raza** *(Columbus Day)*
November 2	**Day of the Dead**
November 20	**Revolution Day**
December 25	**Christmas Day**

At your service

ACCOMMODATION

In the following list, $ = under US$60; $$ = US$60–100; $$$ = US$100–200; $$$$ = US$200 and above.

Campeche (Area Code 981)

HOTEL AMÉRICA
Calle 10, 252
Tel: 6-45-88
hotelamerica@campeche.com.mx
Converted colonial home, rooms around a patio, good budget choice for downtown location. **$**

HOTEL BALUARTES
Av 16 de Septiembre 128
Tel: 6-39-11; fax: 6-24-10
Facing the sea, with 100 comfortable air-conditioned rooms, swimming pool and restaurant. **$$**

HOTEL DE PASEO
Calle 8, 215
Tel: 1-01-00; fax: 1-00-97
Quiet hotel with inviting restaurant and usual amenities. **$$**

Cancún (Area Code 98)

With 20,000 hotel rooms, many in international hotel chains, Cancún offers plenty of choice. The following list is a brief sample, ranging from luxury five-star accommodations to a budget youth hostel:

ANTILLANO
Av Tulúm and Claveles
Tel: 84-15-32; fax: 84-18-78
www.hotelantillano.com
One of the older and also one of the better economy hotels. **$**

HOTEL CAMINO REAL CANCUN
Blvd Kukulcán 9.5
Punta Cancún
Tel: 83-01-00, in US: 1-800-7-CAMINO
Surrounded by the sea on three sides, truly private balconies, architectural drama. **$$$–$$$$**

CLUB MED
Punta Nizuc, Blvd Kukulcán, Km 22
Tel: 85-29-00
Secluded location with view of hotel row, all the usual Club Med amenities, casual atmosphere. **$$$$**

FIESTA AMERICANA CORAL BEACH
Blvd Kukulcán Km 6
Tel: 83-29-00; in US: 1-800-FIESTA-1
A dazzling all-suite resort. All amenities on site. **$$$$**

HOTEL MARGARITA
Av. Yaxchilan 41
Tel: 84-93-33
Small hotel with friendly bilingual staff. **$$**

Hotel Meliá

HOTEL MELIA CANCUN
Blvd Kukulcán Km 16.5
Zona Hotelera
Tel: 85-11-14; fax: 85-19-63
meliavta@cancun.novenet.com.mx
Tropical modern luxury, with a dramatic atrium. **$$$–$$$$**

MELIA TURQUESA
Blvd Kukulcán Km 13
Tel: 83-25-44; in US: 1-800-336-3542
Small, elegant and very private. A favorite with celebrities. **$$$–$$$$**

Oasis Cancun
Paseo Kukulcán Km 18.5
Tel: 85-08-67; fax: 85-05-22
Set in 12 hectares (30 acres) of manicured grounds, with on-site nine-hole golf course and one of the largest pool expanses in Latin America. **$$$**

Plaza Carrillo's
Calle Clavele, 35
Tel: 84-12-27
One of the first downtown hotels. Clean and well maintained. **$$**

Hotel Randall
Av Tulum, 49 at Cobá, Cancún city
Tel: 84-11-22
Pleasant, low-rise, lots of cool marble surfaces, for the budget-minded. **$$**

Ritz-Carlton Cancun
Retorno del Rey, 36
Zona Hotelera
Tel: 85-08-08; in US: 800-241-3333
Fax: 85-10-15
Traditional Ritz-Carlton Continental elegance and refinement. **$$$$**

Hotel Tankah
Av Tankah, 69
Tel: 84-44-46
Simple lodgings for a modest price. **$**

Tropical Inn
Av Yaxchilán, 31
Tel: 84-30-78
Well maintained hotel with rooms set around pretty courtyard. **$$**

Villa Deportiva Juvenil (Youth Hostel)
Blvd Kukulcán, Km 3.2
Zona Hotelera
Tel: 83-13-37
Economical lodgings located in exclusive hotel zone, consisting of dormitories divided by gender. **$**

Chichén-Itzá (Area Code 985)

Hotel Dolores Alba
Km 122 Carretera Valladolid-Chichén-Itzá
No phone. For reservations, contact its sister hotel, the Hotel Dolores Alba in Mérida, tel: (99) 28-56-50, clearly specifying that you want a room at the Chichén-Itzá hotel.
Modest, clean rooms, restaurant with moderately priced meals, pool, 1½ km (1 mile) from ruins. **$**

Hotel Hacienda Chichen-Itza
Zona Arqueológica
Tel: 24-21-50; in US: 1-800-624-8451.
Stay in one of the bungalows. This hotel was once the home of a famous archeologist. **$$**

Hotel Mayaland
Zona Arqueológica
Tel and fax: 1-00-77
Dignified, old-fashioned hotel, pool, with 3 restaurants, 92 units including 12 Mayan villas. **$$$**

Hotel Villa Arqueologica
Zona Arqueológica
Tel: 6-28-30
Club Med amenities – library, restaurant serving excellent food, attractive rooms, almost next to ruins. **$$**

Cozumel (Area Code 987)

Hotel Casa del Mar
Carretera a Chankanaab Km 3
Tel: 2-19-00
Great swim-up bar, plus on-site dive shop and pier. **$$–$$$**

Fiesta Americana Cozumel Dive Resort
Carretera a Chankanaab Km 7.5
Tel: 2-26-22; in US: 1-800-FIESTA-1
Luxury right at fabulous Palancar reef, fabled international diving destination. **$$$**

Hotel Flamingo
Calle 6 Norte, 81
San Miguel
Tel: 2-12-64; in US: 1-800-806-1601
Attractive, quiet rooms a short distance from main plaza at budget prices. **$**

Hotel on Isla Mujeres

GALAPAGO INN
Carretera a Chankanaab Km 1.5
Tel: 2-11-33; US tel: 1-800-847-5708
An expert staff make this a favorite with divers. **$$$**

HOTEL HOLIDAY INN COZUMEL REEF
Carretera a Chankanaab, Km 7.5
Tel: 2-26-22
Luxury close to Palancar reef. **$$$**

HOTEL MELIA MAYAN PARADISUS
Carretera Costera Norte Km 5.8
Tel: 2-04-11
Fax: 2-15-99
Secluded setting on a very long and pretty beach. Luxurious lobby and rooms, all with an ocean view. Pricey, but all inclusive. Book early to ensure space. **$$$$**

PRESIDENTE INTER-CONTINENTAL
Carretera a Chankanaab Km 6.5
Tel: 2-03-22; tel in US: 1-800-327-0200
Ideal for snorkeling. Spacious rooms and deluxe amenities. **$$$$**

HOTEL SAFARI INN
Av Rafael Melgar between Calles 5 and 7, San Miguel
Tel: 2-01-01
A prime budget choice. Pleasant rooms, adjoining dive shop premises. **$**

SOL CABAÑAS DEL CARIBE
Carretera Santa Pilar, Km 4.5
Tel: 2-00-17
Small, but all the amenities of the Spanish chain. A favorite with divers. **$$$–$$$$**

TAMARINDO BED & BREAKFAST
Calle 4 Norte, 421
Tel: 2-36-14
Downtown, simple, colorful, friendly and very comfortable. **$**

Isla Mujeres (Area Code 987)

HOTEL MARTINEZ
Madero, 14
Tel: 7-01-54
Fan-cooled, simple rooms, in small older-style hotel. **$**

HOTEL NA-BALAM
Zazil-Ha, 118
Tel: 7-02-79; fax: 7-04-46
Quiet location for 12 junior suites with ocean views. Restaurant, bar, pool. **$$**

POC-NA
Matamoros and Carlos Lazo
Tel: 7-00-90
Pleasant, well-run youth hostel, for very cheap stay in unisex dormitories. **$**

PERLA DEL CARIBE
Av Madero 2, downtown
Tel: 7-04-44; in US: 1-800-258-6424
Fax 7-00-11
Comfortable, air-conditioned rooms with balcony. Restaurant, bar, pool. **$$**

POSADA DEL MAR
Rueda Medina 15-A
Tel: 7-00-44; in US: 1-800-221-6509
Fax: 7-02-66
Comfortable rooms with a sea view. Restaurant, pool. **$**

Mérida (Area Code 99)

CARIBE
Calle 59, 500 & Calle 60
Tel: 24-90-22
Lovely historic building on attractive plaza downtown. **$$**

CASA DEL BALAM
Calle 60, 48
Tel: 24-21-50
balamhtl@finred.com.mx

Gran Hotel, Mérida

Upscale colonial decor on lively Calle 60. Restaurant, bar, and small pool. **$$–$$$**

CASA MEXILIO
Calle 68 No 495
Tel: 28-25-05
A bed and breakfast with wonderfully eclectic decor. **$$**

CASA SAN JUAN BED & BREAKFAST
Calle 62, 545A
Tel: 23-68-23
csanjuan@sureste.com
Beautifully restored 18th-century house, Three blocks from the main square. Rooms have air conditioning and/or private bath. Rate includes breakfast. **$**

FIESTA AMERICANA MÉRIDA
Av Colón 451
Tel: 42-11-11; in US: 1-800-FIESTA-1
Built to resemble one of the city's colonial-era mansions. Excellent restaurant, bar, pool, tennis. **$$–$$$**

GRAN HOTEL
Calle 60, 496
Tel: 23-69-63/24-77-30; fax: 24-76-22
19th-century grandeur, some rooms with exterior views. **$$**

HACIENDA KATANCHEL
Carretera a Cancún Km 25.5
Tel: 23-40-20
A restored 17th-century hacienda, 15 minutes from Merida. **$$$$**

HOTEL HOLIDAY INN
Av Colón, 498, at Calle 60
Tel: 25-68-77
Chain hotel offering good service, mainly catering to business market. **$$$**

Uxmal (Area Code 99)

HACIENDA TEMOZON
Temozón, 35km from Mérida
Tel: 49-50-01
Spacious, lovely rooms in former hacienda. There are ceiling fans and air conditioning, plus spa, gym, and two natural wells; tours organized. **$$$$**

HOTEL HACIENDA UXMAL
Carretera Mérida-Uxmal Km 78

Telephoning can be thirsty work

Tel: 28-08-40; in US: 1-800-235-4079
Fax: 25-00-87
This is Uxmal's oldest and most traditional hotel. **$$$**

VILLA ARQUEOLOGICA
Ruinas Uxmal
Tel: 28-06-44
Usual Club Med amenities, adjoins the ruins. **$$**

HOTEL MISION PARK INN UXMAL
Carretera Mérida-Uxmal Km 78
Tel: 23-22-02
Very modern hotel, with sweeping view of Uxmal. **$$**

HEALTH AND EMERGENCIES

Make sure you take out adequate medical insurance before leaving home. Once in Mexico, take the usual precautions to avoid stomach upsets. In particular, wash your hands before meals – easy to forget when caught up in traveling. If you are taken sick, immediately inform the staff at your hotel. They will call for medical assistance, sending doctors directly to your room. If hospitalization is necessary, the attending physician can assist you.

Hospitals in some of Yucatán's main cities include:

Cancún – Hospital Americano (tel: 84-61-33); Total Assist (tel: 4-80-82); **Cozumel** – Hospital General (tel: 6-09-20); **Mérida** – Hospital General O'Horan (tel: 24-41-11); Instituto Médico Quirúgico del Sureste (tel: 25-81-64).

COMMUNICATIONS AND NEWS

Media

Some helpful bilingual publications are *Yucatán Today*, a tourist guide you can pick up in hotels. *Discover Yucatán* is a pocket-size free magazine published by the Yucatán Department of Tourism, with brief articles in five languages. *Cancún Tips* is a small-format semi-annual publication available in either Spanish or English, packed with information. All of these tourist-oriented periodicals have maps, the names and telephone numbers of restaurants, hotels, airlines and so on. *Caribbean News* is a colorful bilingual newspaper published bi-monthly in Cancún, which has timely articles as well as useful tourist information.

Museum mask

Telephone / Fax

Mexico's telephone company, Telmex, has installed Ladatel phones almost everywhere. Ladatel phone cards in 30, 50 and 100 peso denominations are avaialable at newsstands and convience stores. Coin-operated phones that take 1, 2 and 5 peso coins are for local and collect calls only. For directory information, dial 040 and prepare your Spanish; for the long distance operator for calls within Mexico, dial 020; for the international operator, dial 090. To dial direct, for calls within Mexico, first dial 01, then the area code and number; for calls to the US and Canada, dial 001, and for other countries, dial 00. If this sounds too complicated, use a "Caseta de Larga Distancia," there's one in almost every town.

USEFUL INFORMATION

Websites

There are numerous websites on Yucatán and Cancún, but check out the following:
www.go2.cancun.com
www.yucatan.gob.mx
www.cancun.com.mx
www.cancunalltours.com

Travel Agencies

Most hotels have an in-house travel agency and every destination (except Campeche) has a wide variety of other travel agencies. In **Campeche**: **Viajes Potoncham**, Calle 67, 1B (tel: 6-67-96), very helpful staff; also **Viajes Campeche**, Calle 10, 339 (tel: 6-08-41). In **Cozumel**: **Turismo Aviomar**, Av 5 between Calles 2 and 4 and in the **Fiesta Inn** and **Coral Princess hotels** (tel: 2-05-88). Efficient service in convenient downtown location.

Tours

Cancún – **American Express**, Av Tulúm 208, (tel: 84-19-99) and **Viajes Thomas Moore**, Playa Langosta (tel: 5-01-44). Excursions to the major destinations accessible from Cancún, plus a variety of water sports services. **Aqua Tours**, Blvd Kukulcán Km 6.25, in front of the Dos Playas Hotel (tel: 83-11-37) and **Royal Yacht Club**, across from the Omni Hotel (tel: 85-03-91) offer a full range of tour options, plus watersports.
Mérida – There are special tours to former *haciendas* and convents. Check with the travel agency in your hotel or contact **Ceiba Tours**, Av Colón, Hotel Holiday Inn (tel: 24-44-77) or **Mayaland Tours**, Av Colón and Calle 60, Plaza Americana 1-A (tel: 23-90-61). **Ecoturismo Yucatán,** Calle 3, 235, 32-A and 34 Pensiones (tel: 25-21-87) for tours to wildlife reserves and general travel requirements.

SPORTS

Bullfighting is popular throughout Mexico and can be experienced at the Plaza de Toros in various cities. Check with your hotel to see if *corridas* are in season at the time of your trip and obtain information on acquiring tickets.

Cancún has the most watersports facilities: the **Aqua Tours**, Blvd Kukulcán Km 6.25 in front of the Dos Playas hotel (tel: 83-11-67) offers a full range of options, plus other watersports, as does **Royal Yacht Club**, Blvd Kukulcán, Km 16.5, in front of the Royal Mayan/Omni hotels (tel: 85-03-91).

Fishing: Mundo Marina and Mauna Loa, above, offer sport fishing trips, including charters.

Diving, snorkeling and scuba: Calm waters of the hotel beaches are great for beginners and children to learn basic snorkel techniques and all have lifeguards. The city's many marinas offer snorkeling and scuba excursions: try **Aqua Tours**, Blvd Kukulcán Km 6.25, in front of the Dos Playas Hotel (tel: 83-11-37) and **Scuba Cancún**, Blvd Kukulcán Km 5.2, across from Lobster Beach (tel: 83-10-11, scuba@cancun.com.mx).

For the more advanced, the Belize barrier reef begins (or ends) its 250-km (155-mile) length near the Club Med at Punta Nizuc. As all beaches are open to the public in Cancún, you could head there to enjoy the sights in the clear shallow water. Cancún is not the most scenic diving spot on the peninsula – Cozumel has that honor – but you can still enjoy yourself.

Isla Mujeres is a favorite nearby diving destination – check with **Scuba Cancún**, Blvd Kulkulcán, Km 5 (tel: 3-14-88), who offer certification courses and have the only decompression chamber in the city.

Cozumel has over two dozen dive shops. **Prodive Cozumel** offers international brands of diving equipment, tours and a private scuba school at several locations: store – Av Adolfo Rosado Salas, 198 (tel: 2-41-23); diveshop – Av 5 and Adolfo Rosado (tel: 2-02-21), with another outlet at the Hotel Fiesta Americana Cozumel Reef Beach Club, Carretera Chankanaab, Km 7.5 (tel: 2-26-22).

FURTHER READING

Incidents of Travel in Yucatán, by John Stephens, illustrations by Frederick Catherwood, Dover, 1969. One of the best reads you'll find, by the renowned 19th-century American explorer.

Lost Cities of the Maya, by Claude Baudez and Sydney Picasso, Thames and Hudson/New Horizons, 1992. Beautifully illustrated account of the explorers, writers, artists and photographers who uncovered the mysteries of the Maya.

Mysteries of the Mexican Pyramids, by Peter Tompkins, Thames and Hudson, 1987. Intriguing read about different pre-Hispanic cultures, plus juicy historical bits.

The Rise and Fall of Maya Civilization, by J Eric Thompson, University of Oklahoma Press, 1986. Brilliantly written and intended for the general reader.

Yucatán Before and After the Conquest by Friar Diego de Landa, Dover, 1978. Written by the priest famously responsible for burning the Mayan codex books in the mid-1500s, this is the most complete description of Mayan customs of its time.

The last boat home

Index

A, B

C

D, E, F

G, H, I

J, K, L

M, N, O

P, Q

R, S, T

U, V, W

X, Y, Z

ACKNOWLEDGMENTS

Photography Marcus Wilson Smith *and*
13 The Antonio García Collection
10, 11 Museo Nacional de Antropología, Mexico City
Front Cover Mireille Vautier
Back Cover E Martino

Editor Erica Brown
Handwriting V Barl
Cover Design Tanvir Virdee
Cartography Lovell Johns